To my friend Dick Lodewick, Best Wishes! Barbara Corn Patterson

The
Rock House Ranch

My Lazy-A-Bar Days

Barbara Corn Patterson

Cover painting and illustrations by
Louise Ippolito Smith

BARBED WIRE PUBLISHING
LAS CRUCES, NEW MEXICO

Published by Barbed Wire Publishing
270 Avenida de Mesilla
Las Cruces, New Mexico 88005 USA

Cover painting and illustrations by Louise Ippolito Smith
Book and cover design by Vicki Ligon.
Fonts used in this book are ITC Berkeley Old Style® and ITC Legacy Sans®.

First printing: September 2002.
Printed in the United States of America.

ISBN #0-9711930-8-8

1   2   3   4   5

DEDICATED TO MY FAMILY

My Parents
Bertha and Irwin Corn

My Children
Carolyn P. Sidd
Ernest Patterson
Ken Patterson
Jim Patterson

My Grandchildren
Amy Sidd
Owen Sidd
Anna Sidd
Heather Patterson
Matthew Patterson
Ryan Patterson

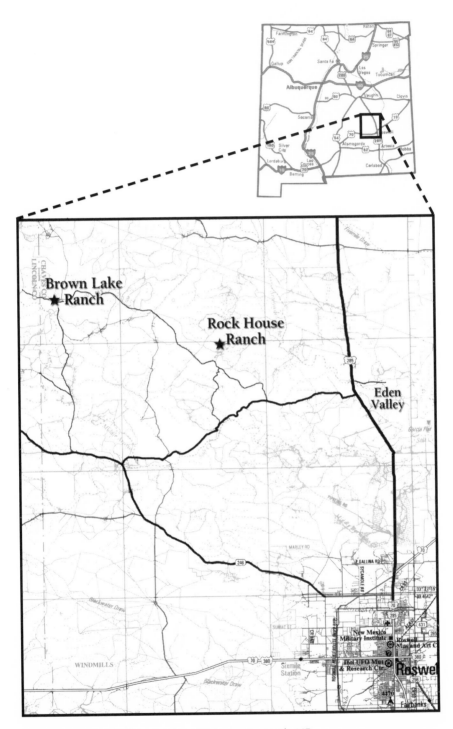

Inset map reproduced with permission of DeLorme, Yarmouth, ME.

Table of Contents

My parents, Irwin and Bertha Corn.

Preface

I have lived between the frontier days and the space age. When I was about nine, I went to San Antonio with my parents to pick up my Grandmother Corn, who had been visiting some of her relatives still living near where she had been raised as a child. I was introduced to her aunt, who was more than ninety years old at the time. She was confined to a day bed by a big bay window so she could look out at the people passing by. I sat beside her and held her thin bony hand. Her skin was milk-white and her voice weak, but she managed to tell me the hair-raising story of how she had been chased by Comanches on the way home from school when she was only seven. I have never forgotten her vivid description and the fear in her voice with the retelling.

I have heard the world is made up of two kinds of people: pioneers and settlers. It seems most of my roots have come from pioneers. At least they were the most interesting to me. My mother's family came to New England in 1632 while my father's folks started out in Virginia in the late 1500's. They seemed to keep moving west every few generations until they ended up in southeastern New Mexico in and around Roswell.

Dad's family came from Kerrville, Texas, in a wagon train in 1878. One of his grandfathers had been killed in Texas by Indians. Mama's widowed grandmother came by wagon in 1901 with her two daughters after the rest of my Roswell ancestors were already here. My mother and father were both born while New Mexico was still a territory.

My family has left me a rich legacy. My mother spent all of her adult life working on our families' genealogy. I admire her dedication and perseverance. There are times I can still hear Mama's voice in my brain telling me to do or not to do something. "Think, think, think," was her main theme of instruction. My mother taught me to use my imagination, to work hard, and to play when the work was done. She was a fantastic role model.

My father talked less, but his example of good living was a strong influence. He was a gentleman, and always was loving and affectionate to Mother. He helped around the house before it became fashionable. I learned things such as to wipe my feet before coming into the house, to help others, never take something that is not yours, be kind to people and animals, and to always close gates. I watched as he and other ranchers bought and sold goods worth many thousands of dollars on a handshake. Once, when someone had taken unfair advantage of him, he said, "Well, if they can live with it, I can live without it."

He and Mother both stressed being independent and self-reliant. Never put yourself above or before others; always respect the other person, especially those who have less or must work harder than you; own up and take responsibility for your mistakes; and above all, be fair and honest.

My parents had rigid rules of finance, too. Don't buy something you can't afford, take care of what you have, and don't waste. Borrow only if absolutely necessary, then pay it back before you spend any on yourself. Interest is why the rich get richer and the poor get poorer.

The only job I was paid for as a child was twenty-five cents to clean the chicken house every other month. I gathered wool from dead sheep in the winter when the snakes were hibernating and the smell was not quite as bad, then sold each tightly packed burlap bag for about two dollars. A heifer calf was branded for me each year, so I had a small herd of cattle when I married just out of high school. Living and learning so many useful things on the ranch has helped me to realize I could accomplish whatever I really worked at.

My parents had applied for a cattle brand for me when I was only six years old. Some of my Long aunts, Dorothy, Frances, and Arline, had thought of the perfect one for me, Bar-Bar-A: two lines over the letter A, which spelled out my name, Barbara. The New Mexico Livestock Board issued LAZY-A-BAR instead. It was the letter A lying sideways with a line below it. I took great pride in it and thought, "I'll bet Shirley Temple wishes she had a brand."

After I received my official LAZY-A-BAR certificate in the mail, my Long aunts made a replica of it across my back with inch-wide adhesive tape. By the end of the summer, I had a white brand on an otherwise well-tanned back. My aunts enjoyed taking me around to neighbors and friends, showing it off.

I still keep my LAZY-A-BAR brand registered more than sixty years later, even though I haven't owned horses or cattle for several years. I now use it as my e-mail address. I could sell it, but I won't. I suppose it has become part of my identity.

Roswell was a nice town to grow up in during my school days. It was safe and people were good. How blessed I am to have had all this, and much, much more in my life since childhood. The sad part is many of my friends and family are no longer still here to share the memories of the good times we have lived.

Recently my present ran smack-dab into my past when I found myself driving my grandchildren through the streets of my childhood, pointing out who had lived where and recounting various incidents, such as the time my neighborhood playmates and I had blocked off a street with the city's wooden barriers so we could play roller-skate hockey using empty milk cans for pucks. (The barriers had been left in the alley by sanitation workers when they went home at five o'clock.)

My mother and grandmothers had done the same sort of reminiscing with me riding in the back seat of the car years before. I wish they had written something of their everyday lives for future generations to have a better understanding of their past, so I'm writing my story so those who follow may get a feeling of ranch life during my childhood. Times change quickly, but people stay much the same.

I recalled my elderly aunt's story about being chased by the Indians again the first time I shook hands with Harrison "Jack" Schmitt, one of our astronauts who had recently returned from walking on the moon on the Apollo 17 mission. I marveled at the scope of my lifetime experiences from her primitive time until the present. I felt that I had one foot in the 19th century and the other in the 21st.

Barbara Corn Patterson
2002

In the beginning...

Acknowledgements

I am deeply grateful to my cousin Helen Reynolds Wright for having faith in me and for helping to edit my book. Also, to my friend Louise Ippolito Smith for the illustrations and the cover painting. My thanks to my family and friends who helped and encouraged me along the way.

The Rock House Ranch

My parents lived in my grandparents' old white frame home place at Eden Valley near the Macho Draw, north of Roswell, New Mexico, when they first married in the summer of 1928. It was referred to as the "Weaning House" since most of Dad's brothers and their wives had lived there briefly after they married.

My folks bought the Rock House Ranch several miles further west in 1937, when I was three years old. It was comfortably situated on a flat expanse of land nested among a ring of large rocky hills divided only by a dry riverbed. You had no warning the ranch was there until you topped a steep hill and looked down upon a small house that had been built of rocks put together with mud and grass straw in 1915. It had been used as a bunkhouse, as well as storage for salt and feed before my parents bought the ranch from my grandparents. Years later my father told a friend who had asked how he had found the secluded ranch in the first place, "You just had to be born there."

The rock house was a long one-room building with a shed-type roof and two doors on the same side of the house. A wood burning cook-stove sat at one end and a bed at the other. There was

A painting of the Rock House Ranch, by Sidney Redfield

a small window at each end of the house. The original floor had been dirt, but concrete had been poured years before we moved into it temporarily, while Dad and a self-taught carpenter built us a house nearby. Dad said he and his brother, Alton, had hauled sand and gravel to build the floor from miles away down the Macho Draw in a horse-pulled wagon.

Dad was not much of a carpenter but did his best. He built by tradition. Both bathroom doors were small and low. My father and all the men in his family were tall, so they would bump their heads if they forgot to duck. Once in a while one of them would forget, bump, and swear. In later years I asked Dad why the doors were so low. He said most old houses had bathrooms added on and had low doors. He simply thought they were supposed to be that way. Our kitchen cabinets were built high to accommodate his six-foot stature even though Mama was not as tall. I had to stand on a stool to do dishes for years.

My very first memory is of my small, white wrought-iron bed that had been passed down at least one generation being moved around in the rock house during a violent thunderstorm to protect me from the leaking roof. "Wake up, Irwin," my mother said as she shook my father. "The roof's leaking and we're going to have to move Barbara's bed. I think she's getting wet."

Dad got out of bed to help. "Here's a dry spot, Bertha," he said, still half asleep. "This should do."

I also remember the construction of our new, small frame house next to the old rock structure. My chores included picking dry walnut shells out of the sand that had been hauled from the creek before it was used to plaster the exterior.

Another was to help put finishing nails into a big bar of soft laundry soap so they would be easier to drive into the hard oak floorboards. Later I helped my parents sand the floor on hands and knees. It had to be "dance floor" smooth.

I am sure some of my "work" was designed to help keep me in sight and safe from the numerous deadly rattlesnakes that frequented the area. Dad told of finding a large rattler coiled and ready to strike only a few feet from where I was playing while they were building our house. My mother said numerous coyotes also came there for water in those days, since it was the only well for many miles. A playful roadrunner would carry my small brightly colored marbles off if I left them outside.

Our new house was not fancy but it was comfortable. It had two bedrooms, a large living room, and a kitchen. The bathroom was between the bedrooms, but because of the Depression, my folks couldn't afford to buy expensive plumbing fixtures. Instead, they built a new outhouse with a large hole for adults and a small hole for me so I wouldn't fall in, a fate worse than death, I could imagine. Indoor plumbing came a few years later.

Until then, baths were taken in the number three washtub in the middle of the kitchen, which was the warmest room in the house. I always got to be first.

Not long after we had moved into our new house, I wandered away from home. Mama thought I was outside with Dad, and he thought I was inside with her. It was a long time before I was missed and their frantic search began. They checked the house, all of the outbuildings, and around the corral, but no Barbara. A young boy had frozen to death not far from our ranch a few years before after he had gone to sleep under a bush. A large search party failed to find him until it was too late.

Irwin Corn with his trademark grin

It was warm weather when I disappeared, but there were still many places a small child could fall or be hidden from sight. My worried parents were about to go get the men from the Civilian Conservation Corps (CCC), who were building a fence a few miles away, to help look for me, when a trapper rode in carrying me and my small dog on his saddle. He had found us walking a couple of miles up the road where I was innocently on my way to Uncle Ronald's ranch. Mama said she cried with relief when I appeared unharmed. Her fear of losing me was intensified because she'd had to wait six long years after they were married before I was born.

The kitchen stove was wood-burning, as was the heater in the living room. It was the only heat we had in the house. Butane stoves had replaced them by the time I started to school. We had no electricity. At first we used kerosene lamps, then later butane or propane gas lights. The only problem was having to turn them off soon after it got dark in the early summer, because an influx of Miller moths would fly into the light and break the fragile glowing mantles.

Our first refrigerator was powered by kerosene until we were blessed with liquid petroleum gas. The old Servel didn't hold much compared to refrigerators today, but it certainly was better than the old ice-box. I barely remember my parents having to haul blocks of ice from town wrapped tightly in a tarp and Mama draining the water pan in the bottom every morning so it didn't run over.

Mama played a great joke at the ranch one year. Dad would come in from working outside, open a Coke, take a couple of swallows, press the cap back on, and return it to the refrigerator. The next time he came in he would take another drink from the bottle. This time Mama replaced the last of his soda with cold leftover coffee, almost identical in color. He took a big swig of that and had the strangest look on his face before he swallowed the bitter liquid.

"What the heck was that?" he asked in astonishment.

"April Fool!" Mom and I called out in unison. Dad finally joined in our laughter.

Some of the neighboring ranches had wind-charger mills that generated 32-volt electricity. My mother held out for a 120-volt power plant instead. She reasoned that having to buy special household appliances which couldn't be used in town, the danger of having hazardous acid storage batteries around, plus the fact that most of the ranch wives who already had wind-chargers

Water in the creek—a rare photo indeed.

found them inadequate, made them less than desirable.

Dad bought a gasoline generator while I was in high school, but still always wanted the lights off at nine o'clock. I don't think poor lighting was much of a problem because Dad believed in being up at dawn and going to bed with the chickens. This habit continued even after electricity. Our house was cold in the winter and hot in the summer. It had no insulation. We just opened or closed windows and doors. That's what everyone did.

Water from our windmill was pumped into a small, elevated storage tank to provide enough pressure to run into the house. The overflow ran into the large rock stock tank that Grandpa Corn had built when the well was drilled in 1915. The water contained many minerals. Mama said, "It was too hard to cook beans." We had a deep, plastered cistern to collect rainwater from the roof for cooking and drinking. It first had the taste and tan color of the new cedar shingles, but soon was clear and wonderful to drink.

I had to turn the crank-handle many a round. It seemed each time I stepped through the kitchen door after I was large enough to carry even half a bucket of water Mama would say, "Barbara, go fill the water bucket." The older I got, the less fun it was.

We had a metal dipper that was always in the water bucket sitting next to the sink on the high kitchen cabinet. Everyone drank from it and put it back for the next person. This was the custom on all of the ranches when I was a child. In town we all shared the same water glass. This was much safer than taking a few quick gulps of opaque brown liquid from a hat brim after scooping it up from a muddy stock tank or a debris-filled water hole where all of the animals in the pasture waded out and drank. That's exactly what we did on roundups. No one ever seemed to get sick; I guess we built up immunity.

Our large square kitchen was where everyone sat during the day. It was a light, bright, friendly room and always smelled good. Mama had painted Grandma Corn's old hand-me-down oak table and ladder-back kitchen chairs fire engine red, which was later followed by canary yellow, then a bright blue enamel. At mealtime the table was always covered with a cheerful, freshly ironed cotton print tablecloth.

Our bright Fiesta dishes were my mother's pride and joy, one of the few things we had that was not second or third hand. I always set the cobalt blue dinner plate at my place. Mama got the green one, since it was her favorite color. My little brother, Tommy, who sat on the kitchen stool next to Mama, usually had a small light blue plate unless I was angry with him; he then received cream color, the least vivid. I usually set an orange place setting for Dad since he'd said he didn't have a favorite color.

The kitchen cabinet top was also painted to match the table. The walls and cabinets were always white. A brightly colored design in the linoleum floor completed the cheerful kitchen decor. Mama sewed white cotton muslin curtains. Once she stenciled cattle brands along the edge. They were inexpensive but attractive. She could always make something nice out of almost nothing.

We always had a calendar hanging beside the back door. It served as a record of when a calf was born or when a nest full of eggs were supposed to hatch. Rainfall and snow measurements were also recorded. Dad made note of the number of calves branded, sheep sold, when the milk cow had been bred, and other important events, such as birthdays and appointments. These all-inclusive accounts were kept for years, and sometimes referred to when questions came up. Mama measured Tom and me every year near our birthday on the door-frame facing the kitchen next to my bedroom. It was interesting to see how much we had grown each year.

I played outside most of the time. One day I was busy driving nails into a crude old homemade table, which had been retired from the rock house to be hauled away with the trash barrel on Dad's next trip to the dump. I had several small nails in my shirt pocket and was busy hammering them into the loose boards so I could "fix" the table. Every now and then I heard a slight noise under the table.

I kept on pounding, thinking the sounds were nails falling from my pocket. Finally, I ran out of nails and bent over to pick up the spilled ones. Right there by my feet was a small rattlesnake; it had been making the noise I was hearing. My reaction to the fear of snakes was so instilled, I ran yelling, "Snake! Snake!" all the way to the house. Dad came running and killed it: another close call.

We were very happy in our new home. Mama always kept the hard oak floor in the living room polished with Johnson's paste wax. I helped rub it with soft clean rags. It was covered with color-ful Navajo throw rugs. The room was light and bright with large windows on the east and south side. The walls were made of light-ly stained plywood. There was a hook in the center of the ceiling to hang a lantern.

Mama had created our living room drapes out of monk's cloth made from new wool sacks. They went well with the rest of the southwest decor. We had a plain brown fabric-covered sofa which had replaced the old cracked leather horsehair-filled one they had brought from Eden Valley. The new one made into a bed when we had company. Our chairs were all old rocking chairs my parents had brought with them also, so no telling how old they were. They were comfortable.

Mama had a small "whatnot cabinet" with glass shelves that held a few dainty treasures. I liked the little brass dog best. She had hung a cluster of brightly painted gourds and a few framed western prints on the walls. My household chores as a child were to pick up my room, empty waste baskets, shake the rugs, and dust the furniture.

Our bookcase held a nice collection of well-read books as well as an always rotating shelf of newly purchased or borrowed ones. My brother Tommy and I had some of ours on the bottom shelf: *Tom Sawyer*, *Little Women*, *Treasure Island*, assorted Nancy Drew mysteries, *Alice in Wonderland*, and *Mother West Wind*, to name a few. We also had comics which had been passed around from our cousins and Uncle Pat. Mama looked these over to set aside the "bad" ones before we could read them. *Donald Duck*, *Superman*, and *Wonder Woman* were all right. Mother read to me almost every after-noon at nap time before I started to school.

Our battery radio was on a corner table in the front room. We listened for the news at noon, and again at night for entertaining programs such as *Amos and Andy*, *Lux Theater*, and *The Grand Old Opry*. We always had to be careful not to run the batteries down. We played cards, dominoes, or worked jigsaw puzzles while we lis-tened every night after supper. Sometimes Tommy and I would build houses with his Lincoln Logs and make windmills with the Tinkertoy set.

The floors of both bedrooms and the kitchen were covered

with slick linoleum. They were cool in the summer but downright freezing in the winter. I had a small Navajo rug by my bed until Dad needed it for a saddle blanket, then I used a blue cotton shag rug Grandma Corn had given me for my birthday. The bedrooms were closed off to save the heat in the rest of the house, so I always dreaded going to bed in the winter. Tommy and I slept together when we were children; we helped keep each other warm even though sometimes we fought.

"Mama, Mama, Barbara kicked me," Tommy called out.

"But he's on my side," I replied in defense.

"You kids settle down and go to sleep," was the usual retort.

Our bedroom was on the northwest corner of the house with a large window on each outside wall. Ice would be on the inside glass some mornings. Mama said, "Just look! Jack Frost came during the night and painted the window with delicate icy designs." Our folks would fill a hot water bottle for us when it was really cold. It felt wonderful. Tom and I took turns dressing in the living room in front of the stove where our clothes were already neatly laid out and warm.

Breakfast was usually ready before my brother and I were called to get up. We always had fried bacon and eggs, hot cereal with plenty of thick cream, and toast or biscuits with butter and jam. Mom and Dad could both mix biscuits right on top of a large bag of flour or in the bin without even measuring or using a bowl. They just poured a little of this and that in and carefully worked their fingers around the sticky dough until it was gently placed on the bread board to be rolled out and cut into nice large biscuits.

Sometimes I helped put them into the pan with a little bacon grease to keep the "little turtles," as Dad called them, from sticking. There was usually a jar of thick molasses that my father poured over a piece of bread while it was still hot from the oven. Other times we would have thick cream gravy over a biscuit when Mama cooked pork chops or sausage.

There was a small "shot" glass in the center of the table with the salt, pepper, and sugar bowl. It had a Democrat donkey on it and the Roosevelt campaign logo, "Happy Days Are Here Again,"

Irwin & Bertha Corn

even though my family and most of the other ranchers were Republicans. It held small round, fiery hot, dried red chili petines. My father and uncles crushed and sprinkled them with their fingers on almost everything except their salads and desserts. One tiny pod would spice up a large pot of frijole (pinto) beans. Uncle Ronald once made the mistake of rubbing his eye after he had touched the hot chili and sat with tears in his eyes for the rest of the meal. I knew not to touch them.

Dad had learned to cook when he had to stay alone at the ranch and sheep camp as a young man. He started almost everything he cooked by frying bacon, followed by sliced onions, hot green chiles, then added a vegetable, potatoes, or eggs. His cabbage and squash dishes were my favorites. We had fresh ham or pork chops in the winter to supplement the beef or mutton we had year round. The rich food didn't seem to harm their health. Mama died the day before her eighty-third birthday of emphysema, after smoking for sixty-five years. Dad just wore out when he was ninety.

Once when I was up at Aunt Margaret and Uncle Alton's ranch they gave me some half-grown kittens. We needed a barn cat to keep the mouse population down, so Dad agreed to take them home tied in a gunny sack in the trunk of our car. I had wanted one for a long time, but Mama thought I would get ringworm. When we got home, my mother had already gone into the house; I brought the bag of squirming felines into the kitchen and untied the string.

They jumped out and ran in every direction. One climbed right up the monk's cloth drape, and was on top of the curtain rod. The sound of all this brought Mama with the broom. "Barbara Ann, hold the door open." (I knew I was in a lot of trouble when she used my middle name.) She scooted those three cats out the back door in a high run, never to be seen again. Dad laughed, but I knew better than to say a single word.

Mama had a gasoline Maytag washing machine out in the old rock house at the ranch. Dad would pump water from the cistern the night before and get up before daylight to start a fire in the wood cook stove in the rock bunkhouse to heat the wash water. Two number three galvanized washtubs placed on a stand next to the washer were filled with cold water to rinse the clothes. One had bluing added to make the white clothes look whiter. A long exhaust hose carried the smoke and fumes from the "pop-pop" single cylinder motor safely out the door.

I enjoyed helping separate the dirty clothes into piles for each load. First the white clothes, then colored; a load of Levis or home-made rag rugs was always last. Mom used a long smooth stick to pluck each item of clothing carefully up out of the soapy water in the swishing machine. She then lifted it up to the pair of heavy moving rubber rollers to squeeze the wash water out, then put the clothes into the rinse tub. This was repeated with each rinse until the clean laundry was placed into a basket ready to be hung to dry. Mama often cautioned, "Don't get near the wringer. That's how Grandma Corn got her finger cut off." I had seen her short finger and gladly heeded the warning.

Hanging the wet clothes on the long clothesline behind the house was the next step. I couldn't reach the wire, so I would hand Mama one wet item at a time or wooden pins as she slowly worked her way down the line. I was to chase animals away while clothes were hanging because horses and cattle would chew on them if they had a chance. The clean laundry smelled fresh after it had been in the sun and was soft from blowing in the gentle breeze. After the washing was done, I enjoyed playing with my little toy cars and making rivers as the soapy wash water was drained outside the door. Dad carried the rinse water to pour on our few small struggling elm trees.

Part of the time my mother used soap she had made from fat rendered by roasting pork skins in the oven from the pigs we had butchered. The crisp dry pork skins, or "cracklings," which were left after the hot lard was poured off, were eaten as snacks. They were good to chew on while riding horseback. Mama poured the lye soap mixture into a pan to cool, then cut it up in small pieces for her washing. Grandma Long especially liked it for her laundry. Some people still boiled clothes in a wash pot, which really would have been hot, hard work.

Ironing was another full day for my mother. She first sprinkled everything that needed to be pressed, and that included her cotton bras and Dad's boxer shorts. Mama set up her large homemade ironing board using the kitchen table at one end for support and the white schoolteacher chair for the other. It also held the bag of damp clothes. My mother always seemed to know exactly where each piece of clothing was in the ironing bag.

She then placed three or four flat-irons around the largest burner on the stove and heated them; carefully covered with an old black skillet to hold the heat in. Mama used a wooden handle to hook onto one, then lifted it from the fire. She first pulled out one of Dad's old cotton handkerchiefs to test it on to see if it was the right temperature. Sometimes it would smoke and leave a scorched print the shape of the iron. It would just pucker up the soft cloth if the metal wasn't hot enough.

She then guided it carefully over everything in the bag, piece by piece. Mama had to iron fast to take advantage of the heat before it cooled off, then replaced it and continued the painstaking process until the bag was empty. This was an especially hot, hard job in the summer when we had no fan or air conditioning.

I learned to iron on flat easy pieces such as Daddy's cotton handkerchiefs, napkins, and Mama's hand embroidered pillowcases. I stayed outside with the animals most of the time. Mama did the ironing in town after I started to school, since we had electricity there, but she continued to wash at the ranch for many years. She and Grandma both said, "Those new washing machines just don't get clothes as clean." They had the same reluctance to use clothes dryers and other modern appliances later on.

Soon after our new ranch house was built, Dad and I drove to the mountains to get a load of pine lumber from the sawmill at Spindle to build new corrals. It was just a wide spot along the Pine Lodge Road on the north side of the Capitan Mountains. We had borrowed Grandpa Corn's old truck since we only had a car. I loved to hear the sound of the engine as it climbed up the steep inclines through the tall pines. The sawmill was noisy, but had the wonderful aroma of fresh pine.

Mama had sent along crackers, cans of pork and beans, and Vienna sausages for our lunch. Dad and I had our picnic under a tree while the lumber was being loaded, then made our way slowly back down the long dirt road. We spent the night at Aunt Margaret and Uncle Alton's ranch before going on home early the next day.

The same carpenter who had built our house helped build the corral. He and Dad set two tall cedar posts close together for a narrow gate near the barn, but first used them to make me a temporary swing to keep me occupied while they worked. It rained hard one night and the next morning I ran through the mud puddles to the swing about fifty yards from the house. Just as I got to our small barn, which also served as a saddle house, I saw a monster.

I ran back to the house screaming with fear. "Mama, Mama, Mama, there's a big black thing with yellow spots right by my swing!" I had expected them to rush out the door in excitement like they did when I found a snake. Instead they only laughed at me while sitting at the kitchen table calmly drinking coffee, saying what I had seen was only a harmless "waterdog." I knew good and well what I had seen was not any kind of dog. It was years before I saw another salamander and satisfied my curiosity.

I had to entertain myself most of the time. I spent hours climbing the small elm tree outside the kitchen window where Mama could keep an eye on me. Another favorite pastime was to play dress-up with the clothes in Mama's rag-bag. One time I used a crayon to draw a big red "S" on one of her embroidered cup towels made from a white salt-sack. I tied it around my neck, and raced around and around the yard "flying" with Superman at my side.

Dad built a large wooden swing set complete with a monkey-bar and see-saw. Mama hung by her knees and taught me how to spin on the bar. One time I was spinning too fast and the bar fell with me on it. I used a small bag of feed I'd hauled from the barn to tie to the see-saw for a counter balance so I could go up and down. It sort of worked, but what I really needed was someone my age to play with.

When I was eleven, Mom and Dad built a large new living room onto our ranch house so Tom could have their bedroom. They used what had been the old living room for their new bedroom. The new room was long, with a yellow brick fireplace at one end and windows all along each side. It had a view of the windmill and rock tank on the east and the old rock bunkhouse on the west.

One night while the room was only a foundation with subflooring, Tom and I heard our dog, Susie, barking frantically, then heard the loudest buzz from a rattlesnake I have ever heard. Its continuous rattling sounded like a train letting off steam.

Dad got up, pulled on his boots, and went out with his twelve-gage shotgun, clad only in his boxer shorts. I wanted to laugh but was too frightened of the snake. It was on the sub-floor-ing of the new room when he blew it to pieces with double-aught buckshot. I will always remember thinking about snake blood and some of that shot being in the wood under the nice oak flooring which was later placed over it.

Mama bought new western style oak furniture, including a dining room table and chairs, but everyone still sat in the kitchen around the brightly painted table except when we had company for dinner. The old rocking chairs were moved to a screened-in porch, which had also been added on to our house. It was great place to sit and catch the afternoon breeze and read or watch the ever-changing cumulus clouds float by. We often rested or took a siesta after lunch in the hot summertime unless there was pressing work to be done. It helped to break up our long daylight-to-dark work routine. This was home.

It is a wonder Mama didn't run me off the ranch one day when I decided to take my horse into the kitchen. Don't ask me why I did that. It just seemed like a good idea at the time. I was proud I had trained my horse Blanco to follow me anywhere. Mom hurried into the kitchen as soon as she heard the strange clump, clump of the horse's hooves on the hard linoleum floor. She stopped abruptly as soon as she saw us and spoke quietly so she wouldn't startle the horse, "Barbara Ann, get that darned horse out of here before he falls down and breaks a leg." Her tone needed no volume to be clearly understood. Gee, if I had known it would have upset her so, I would not have gone there.

She definitely didn't want critters in her kitchen.

Ranch Work

Families did most of their own ranch work. Children who were old enough did the work of a man. Wives helped; most could do everything their husbands did, plus raise children and chickens and do household chores. Many hauled drinking water and helped with other daily tasks, such as carrying wood, milking, feeding animals, and gathering eggs. Young children helped with whatever they could. Responsibilities came early on a ranch.

Once, before I started to school, I felt something soft under my boot while I was hanging up the empty egg bucket on the yard fence post. It felt like cloth. I looked down and saw that I was standing on a small rattlesnake. I'm sure it must have been as startled as I was. "Snake! Snake!" was all I could say. Dad came and killed it.

After that, Mama bought some guinea hens that were supposed to scare snakes away with their shrill noise. The foxes, skunks, and owls ate most of the birds, and we still had snakes. Another time when I was gathering eggs one evening and reached under a hen who refused to get off her nest, I put my hand on a snake. Now that was a shock! It turned out to be a harmless bull-

snake stealing eggs, but it surely shook me up.

If it wasn't one thing, it was another. Corrals, windmills, fences, and equipment had to be built, painted, or repaired. Vehicles, tools, and machinery had to be serviced. Water troughs had to be drained and cleaned periodically. There was never an end to the work to be done, besides taking care of the critical financial business of ranching.

Family-operated ranches in southeastern New Mexico, just west of the Pecos River, were from twenty-five to fifty sections of land (a section is 640 acres, or one square mile), so each covered a lot of territory. Some ranches were much larger; they needed more than one person or family to do the work. Owning and managing a ranch was a full-time occupation when I was a child, not at all like the movies where the cowboys sat around all day, sang, and played the guitar.

There were chores to do every day. We checked livestock to see that they had plenty of feed, water, and salt, always watching for sick animals and treating them. We rode along countless miles of fence to look for holes that stock could get through or for gates carelessly left open, while all the time observing the ground for tracks that didn't belong. Rustlers and unwanted hunters left car tracks off the roads; coyotes dug under the net-wire sheep-proof fences to move from pasture to pasture killing sheep. We watched for circling buzzards to locate dead animals, which we examined to try to discover their cause of death.

Ranch children were "schooled" in being attentive and resourceful from the time they could ride out into the spacious pastures alone. It was so subtle we never realized we were learning. My parents would ask, "How much water is left in the water hole? Were there many cattle there? How about sheep? Oh, did you see the cow we doctored the other day? Had her calf sucked? Has Ronald been down the road yet? Well, did you see any fresh tire tracks on the road? How many bucks did you see in the house pasture? Any woolies we missed shearing?"

The endless questions were never asked all at once, but by the time the day was out my memory had been taxed. I dared not confess I had mostly been preoccupied with daydreaming and watching a comical roadrunner chasing a blue-tailed lizard. I gradually learned to report anything out of the ordinary and to find solutions to any problems that I identified.

I once found a large hole that had been torn in the fence between Uncle Richard's ranch and ours where two bulls had been fighting. I managed to pull and tie it together well enough to keep stock from passing through before I rode home to tell Dad. For once I had done something that would be considered important. My folks duly praised my temporary repair job. I soon learned to check to see if the windmill needed to be tied off to keep it from tearing apart when a rod was broken, or to fix the float on a water trough so the tank wouldn't be drained dry. There was always something to do when you learned to identify needs.

One day Dad and I were out riding when he pointed to a large number of cattle in the distance, too numerous to count individually. "How many cows are there?" he asked. I didn't have a clue. He showed me how to look at them in smaller units of twenty-five or so, and then add the groups to get a totaled estimate. It worked.

Cattle and sheep would both sometimes bog down in the soft deep mud around dirt tanks as they were trying to get to the last small pool of water before it completely dried up. The rancher had to remove his boots, wade out into the mire, tie a rope around the poor distressed animal, then hook the other end around the saddle horn or the car's bumper and pull the poor critter free; otherwise it would struggle until it died. Many an entrapped cow failed to fully appreciate the lifesaving act and, once free of the mud, chased the rescuer. Dad would say, "Barbara, go take the rope off of her neck as soon as I give you some slack, then run and get back on your horse." Believe me, I ran fast!

There was always unglamorous work to be done, which most people do not realize is an important part of ranching. Ice had to be chopped on water troughs and dirt tanks in the winter so stock could drink. I often thought my fingers would freeze and fall off when we had to reach into the water and pitch out the cold chunks of ice.

Feed had to be hauled and left for livestock during the cold winter months and during droughts when there was a shortage of grass. We would take cottonseed meal pellets that we called "cake" out to small herds of sheep or cattle that would quickly gather as soon as Dad honked the horn. Before the winter was over they would come running as soon as they saw or heard our pickup.

My father would lift the eighty-pound burlap bags of thumb-sized cottonseed meal pellets and walk along a smooth path to leave a narrow brown trail of the protein-rich feed behind. Dad had to step lively or the hungry cattle would knock him down. He would pour a bucket of cubes for me to spread when there were only sheep around since they were smaller and less dangerous.

I liked to chew on the animal feed "cubes" even though my mother had scolded me saying, "That stuff isn't clean enough for people to eat. Leave it alone." Dad took me with him to the cotton oil mill to pick up a truck load of the still steaming warm feed early one winter morning. It smelled almost like one of Mama's beef roasts cooking. I stood there watching the thin round pellets moving along on a conveyer belt on their way to the sacking machine, when one of the workers who was inspecting it spat a large squirt of chocolate-colored chewing tobacco juice right on the feed as it passed by. I felt my throat almost gag and never ate it again.

Sometimes we fed a few animals in our stock pens behind our barns. A steer or a fat lamb to be butchered, a mother cow who was weak and needed a boost, or a hospital pen of animals needing special care were the usual collection. We gave them alfalfa hay in addition to the pellets. The green flakes of tender dry leaves were sweet to smell when you first cut the wires holding them together into a tightly pressed bale. The only time I hated to put it into the long feed troughs was when the wind was blowing and would whip up dust and small bits of the feed back into my face and eyes. The most annoying part was having the trash get under my collar and down my shirt. It itched until I could take a bath, which was usually not before bedtime.

Salt troughs as well as supplemental vitamin and mineral blocks had to be placed and monitored near all of the watering places so the stock would maintain a healthy balance of nutrients. At times we would have to drive animals that had been watering around a water hole that had dried up over near a windmill so they would relocate.

Water gaps and fences often had to be rebuilt after a hard rain. At times stock that had passed through the damaged fence had to be rounded up and put back where they belonged. Once we found Mom's horse, Midget, badly trapped and tangled in sharp wire where he had walked across following the rest of the herd. Fortunately the gentle old gelding stood quietly as Dad took wire cutters from the tool box to cut him free.

Uncle Richard had a young palomino mare that had been eating addictive loco weeds and was so crazy acting she tried to run through a fence. The badly injured animal had to be put down. It was always sad to have to shoot an animal, especially horses, since we grew so fond of most of them. Mama poured

If it's not one thing, there's always another. This is a racer snake, stretched out and crawling along the second-to-top wire of a fence!

salt to try to kill the blue green fern-like loco weeds which looked so innocent. Dad said, "Their roots must reach down to China." We also chopped and burned other noxious plants and sticker weeds which grew around water holes and lake beds so the sharp needles wouldn't injure the animals or get into the sheep's wool.

Weather was especially important to ranchers. Our entire livelihood depended upon the precious rain. Mom and Dad watched the sky all of their lives in hopes of moisture. In the summer we would see the majestic giant thunderheads building over the mountains to the west and would closely monitor them as they came nearer and grew larger and darker. Finally, we could smell the fresh scent of falling rain. More often than not the clouds would start to dissipate before they made their way to us. Mama was quite accurate in looking at clouds miles away and judging just where it had rained.

We were sometimes fortunate enough to receive at least a few scattered showers over parts of the ranch. Occasionally the clouds would gather and cover the sky, then burst with a good downpour, bringing enough rain to run off the hills and fill the natural lake beds, water holes, and dirt tanks, providing water for our livestock and reviving the hearty vegetation. It's amazing how quickly the hills turned green with tall grass gently waving in the summer breezes and the difference that transpired as plants and animals began to respond to the welcome moisture. The broad valleys were soon covered with white, yellow, and orange wildflowers. The dainty grama grass hid all but the largest rocks to soften the once harsh hillsides. A good rain always made my folks feel young again. They would dance around the kitchen in a playful mood.

Mama believed in "rain signs." If we saw a snake, tarantula, or a terrapin cross the road she would declare, "It's going to rain." Sometimes it did.

Dad was much more certain with his predictions, "You'll know it's raining when you hear the frogs croaking." Another favorite saying of his was, "It always rains at the end of a long drought."

Once in a while a violent thunderstorm would wake everyone up. Mama would rush around closing windows where the rain might blow in. Lightning would crack and thunder roared. We could see puddles forming in the large open space between the yard and the corrals each time we heard the loud BOOM and saw the bright flash. Sometimes I would be frightened. "Go get on your bed." My mother reassured me. "You'll be safe there." It became my comfort zone for everything, including hurt feelings or a broken heart.

The morning following a rain I would put on my oldest boots to go walk over the hills while the ground was still soft and wet. The air smelled so fresh and clean. This was the only time we would see black and yellow striped millipedes crawling on hundreds of tiny legs. They coiled up into a tight spiral when they were touched. "They won't hurt you," Dad assured me, but they looked a lot like the poisonous centipedes which Mother had cautioned me about, so I left them alone.

The most fascinating insects we found only the first few hours after a rain were the bright red velvet-textured "rain ticks" as we called them. They were rare. We also had large black vinegarroons which looked threatening but were harmless. They only had a bad odor. Their cousin, the scorpion, had a sting that felt as though I had stepped on a red-hot coal when I touched one while going to the bathroom barefooted in the dark one night. We learned to shake our clothes and boots before dressing.

I have always loved to listen to the sound of rain, especially when we would stand in the barn and hear it resounding on the hard tin roof. Every few years it would hail. It made an almost deafening noise. Dad told of a sheepherder and many of his flock being killed by hail years before. I was told to unsaddle my horse and put my head under the saddle in case I was caught out in a hailstorm.

Mama told of how her father had been hit by lightning passing along a steel fence while he was opening a gate. It knocked him down and burned his yellow rain slicker. His young daughter, my Aunt Etta, was with him and helped look for his pipe that had been in his mouth, which they finally found several feet from where he had been hit. "Never ride next to the fence when there is lightning nearby," Mama reminded us many times.

Droughts were the most dreaded part of ranching. When the pastures were lush and green, we seemed to think it would stay that way forever. It would not. The shallow lakes dried up first, soon followed by the water holes. Hot summer winds soon parched the entire countryside. Hopeful eyes followed every cloud that passed by thinking, "Maybe it will rain today."

Brief droughts were manageable. Ranchers expected short dry periods. Stock could be moved to pastures with more grass or fed for awhile. The most difficult time was during a series of dry years which extended over a large area of the country. The only solution was to sell off stock to keep them from starving. First the old and weak were culled to be sold. Soon the livestock markets were flooded with animals and prices plummeted. Calf and lamb crops were short because hungry animals do not breed well, much less produce enough milk to raise fat babies. Many who owed a lot of money had to sell out or were foreclosed by the bank. The hope of rain was all that kept anyone in the ranching business.

Maintaining a critical balance between having enough stock to fully utilize the pasture grasses available, while trying to avoid overgrazing to the extent that the land could be harmed, was a never-ending task. Most ranchers realized they would only hurt themselves in the long run by keeping too many animals on stressed grasslands during droughts. A pasture that had been grazed down almost to the dirt would take much longer to recover than one left with a good stand of dry vegetation. The topsoil would blow away, leaving little to grow but noxious weeds when it did rain.

Many ranches had been in the same families for generations

and would be passed down again and again. Also, there would be little resale value in a ranch that had been overgrazed. It was the crux of the business to protect and preserve the valuable natural resources. Most ranchers had been true ecologists long before they had ever heard the term. They stood to lose their entire livelihood unless they took an active part in protecting the land.

We did without a telephone as well as electricity. One time our nearest neighbors in a radius of about ten miles got together and hooked up a battery-operated crank phone system between ranches, using the top barbed wire above the net-wire fence for the telephone line. We each had a special series of rings to identify our calls. Two longs and one short, or three short rings, and various other combinations told us when to answer. Everyone on the line could listen in if they wished, so there was no privacy. But it was still better than no communication.

Mama gave three deliberate sharp turns to the crank on the side of our old wooden Western Electric telephone mounted on the living room wall. The ding, ding, ding rang into seven other homes and one barn since one old lady on the line wouldn't allow a phone in her house because there were none mentioned in the Bible. Her husband had to be reached either early in the morning or late in the evening while he was doing chores.

"Hello," my Aunt Dorothy's cheerful voice answered. She had expected the call would be for her since the men did most of their telephoning before breakfast or after supper. Their conversations were short and to the point, usually about the weather, to see who had been fortunate enough to have rain, or to plan work when help was needed.

"Hello, Dorothy," my mother replied. "How are you this morning?"

"Oh, I'm just fine, Bertha. And you?"

"We're all right. I just wanted to let you know we were in town yesterday and they have peaches out on East Second Street for two dollars a bushel. They were still a little green, so I didn't buy any."

"That sounds awfully high," she replied. They both heard the distinct click of someone lifting a receiver.

"Hi, it's me, Syble. I just wanted to say hello. I figured it would be you two visiting. I heard you talking about peaches. Richard and the kids and I are going to Ruidoso in a couple of days. Do either of you want us to get you some peaches while we're there?"

"No, Syble, but thanks for asking. We're going up to Taos next week. Their fruit should be coming off about now. Dorothy, are you all going to be able to get away to go with us?"

"I'm afraid not, Bertha. TM said he was going to help the McKnights work on their windmill. Bring me back a bushel if you buy peaches. I've got to go. My potatoes are about to boil over. Bye now."

"Syble, good talking to you too, but I guess I'd best get off the line before I run the batteries down. Goodbye."

These brief encounters helped relieve some of the loneliness ranch wives experienced, being so isolated from all except their immediate family. Sometimes the phone would short out somewhere along the miles of barbed wire and everyone would then have to ride the fence to locate the problem. A primitive system at best, we gave up on it when I started to school.

My mother would take me with her when she walked down the Rock House Draw so she could shoot prairie dogs. They were a menace to ranchers because they ate grass roots and killed large areas of vegetation. All that was left was the bare dusty ground where they popped out of their deeply-dug dens to stand guard. These holes were a hazard to horses and livestock when they walked across the prairie dog towns. Later on, the CCC boys eradicated the harmful rodents. Mama taught me how to carefully aim and shoot her small single shot twenty-two rifle at an early age, but I only watched as she or Dad used the large twelve-gauge shotgun to kill rattlesnakes.

One hot afternoon my father was unloading hay in our closed-in shed. I was standing near the truck while Dad was arranging bales of hay inside the barn, when he suddenly called out, "Barbara! Go get the shotgun out of the truck. There's a rattler in here." I immediately did as I was told.

The gun was heavy compared to Mama's lightweight rifle. My father was trapped inside, with the large tan and black snake tightly coiled and buzzing angrily between him and the one and only door.

"I can't get out. You're going to have to shoot it. Just wait until I get back so you don't hit me."

I was terrified! The shotgun was so heavy I could barely hold it up. Dad finally called from inside, "Okay, now just hold the gun tightly to your shoulder and shoot."

BANG! That old twelve-gauge almost knocked me down. Thank goodness, the snake lay limp with bits of bloody flesh showing. Dad waited a few minutes to be certain it was really dead, then came out and praised my action.

Mama listened intently to my rendition of the snake incident at the supper table that night. "Isn't your shoulder sore?" she inquired, concerned that I may have been injured by the recoil.

"No, it's only a little tender, but that shotgun sure does kick,"

I replied.

Dad added, "The secret to shooting a shotgun is holding it firmly so it won't bounce against your shoulder. Barbara did just fine."

We rarely had hired help. Dad only brought a hired man from town when there was extra work to be done, or while Mama, Tom, and I were in town during school. Most of the hired men on the Corn ranches were single men, partly because we didn't have housing for a family, but mostly because family men needed to have full-time jobs rather than only occasional work. They all liked working for my father because he was mild-mannered and treated them well.

The single ranch hand cowboys all lived with some of their family. Dad would go to their house to see if they would come and work for us. More often than not, they would be either at the Star Bar or in jail. My father picked them up, paid their bills or bail, took them to get their bedroll and a change of clothes, then headed home to the ranch.

It wasn't unusual for these cowboys to borrow money when there was no work. Chapo came to our house in town one afternoon. Mama went to the door and told him, "Irwin isn't here. He's at the ranch."

"Well," the bashful man would hesitate, "I need to borrow some money."

"I don't know when he will come back to town," she stalled knowing full well what the next question would be.

"Can you loan it to me? My sister, she's sick and I have to have money for the doctor," was the sad plea. "I need ten dollars today." Chapo's sad brown eyes were more than even my mother could take.

Finally she handed him a check. "Now, take care of your sister and don't go to the bar!" she admonished. Sure enough his friend called the next day and "needed" fifteen dollars to bail Chapo out of jail. He didn't get it this time. They "worked off" their loans when they went to the ranch.

When Dad came to town and heard the tale he asked, "Why did you loan it to him, Bertha?"

"Because I knew you would have if you had been here," she replied. He knew she was right as usual.

Dad always gave the hired man's family some money in advance on their account before they went to the ranch. He often took meat by their house when we butchered. (He sometimes took a fat mutton to the man who was supposed to run the county's road grader to get our rough ranch road repaired.) There was usually one stop on the way out of town to buy the hired man tobacco. We furnished all of their food, or "chuck" as it was called. It was also our custom to help them out when they got too old to work.

The hired men would go to the ranch for a week, or perhaps even up to two or three months, depending on what work needed to be done. Some would bathe and change into their "town clothes" at the ranch before they came back to town at least once a month. Others would have Dad stop and let them out at the dry-goods store to buy new clothes from the skin out. They would then go to Arnold's Barbershop for a shave, shower and haircut. Now they were ready to go see the "bright lights." The "ladies" and the bars would usually have all that was left of their month's pay before daylight. The cycle of the single cowboy ranch hand would start all over again.

My favorite hired men were Chapo, Roy, and Nabor, who spoke little English. That was no problem because Dad was fluent in Spanish he had learned by spending summers with Mexican sheepherders when he was a boy. Some of the hired men tried to teach me. "Uno, dos, tres," we practiced. They lived in the old rock bunkhouse.

Most of these men were good cooks. Sometimes my mother

let me eat with them. They always had beans, meat, and my favorite, fresh hot tortillas. Sliced tomatoes, green chile, onions, and vegetables in season were welcome additions. Jam or molasses on bread, canned fruit, or a large bowl of sweet rice with raisins completed their rock house meals. Sometimes the men ate in our house with us or filled their plates with food and took it out to their bunkhouse. Nabor let me drink coffee with a lot of milk and sugar. He teased me saying, "Coffee will make your skin dark like mine." I hoped it would.

Nabor was almost deaf. Dad would yell, trying to make him understand. Finally my father bought him a hearing aid. Nabor thought it was wonderful. For some reason he had always called me Maggie, my Grandmother Corn's name. When he could hear, Nabor asked Dad, "Why for you call her Barbara?"

Another day he came out to the barn to work and couldn't hear. Dad asked, "Nabor, where's your hearing aid?"

He said, *"Está en mi casa."*

"¿Por qué? Why aren't you wearing it?"

Nabor responded, "I'm saving the battery so I can listen to the radio at night."

Watching Nabor learn how to drive was another experience. He would rev the engine up until he felt the pickup vibrate, then pop out the clutch in whatever gear it happened to be in, and take off in a cloud of dust. He especially enjoyed showing off his driving skills when another hired man was around. Dad figured Nabor needed to know how to drive in case of an emergency while Mama was in town sending me and my brother to school.

There were times when more than our family was needed to get our work done. My uncles and Dad helped each other work stock when they had to round up or work on a wind-

the hill was moving when quail were plentiful. Mama considered the birds near the house as ours to care for and to use. "What's the difference in taking a few in the trap rather than shooting them and injuring more than you kill," was her logic.

Besides, she was always proud of never having steel "shot" in her birds. She once told Uncle Ray, when he commented on the absence of bird shot as he enjoyed a quail dinner with us, "I always shoot them in the head with my twenty-two." The warden's warning was the last of the trap.

Ranchers had to do most of their own veterinary work. We carried medicine and a rope on our saddles in the summer to catch and treat stock. Screw-worm maggots infested even the smallest wound on an animal, eating on their flesh until the poor animal died, unless caught and doctored with a foul-smelling thick black liquid pine-tar medicine, which was poured into the putrid sore. A small twig or wooden match stick was used to carefully dig out the repulsive squirming larva from the wound one at a time until they had all been removed. It was hard not to gag seeing and smelling these awful greedy insect larvae at work on a pitiful host animal. Thank goodness, they have now been eradicated by dropping sterile flies in the Southwest and Mexico.

Cattle occasionally had to be treated for pinkeye. Getting medicine into the first eye was not so bad, but treating the second one was a real trick. Some old-fashioned ranchers just threw a handful of salt into the cow's eye. All that did was make it water.

Others used yellow powdered sulfur. Dad bought "modern" medicine from the veterinarian. Some of it left a bright blue stain that made it easy to spot the cow again when riding in the pasture to see if her

eyes had improved.

Watching stock closely during lambing and calving was especially important. Sometimes they needed help expelling the fetus; it had to be "pulled." Young ewes and heifers had the most problems with their first deliveries. At times a newborn baby could not get hold of a swollen teat for its first critical meal. Milking a wild cow is not easy.

Once in a while a cow's uterus would prolapse. Dad would have to tie her up, push her insides back into her, then hold them in place using a sawed off broom handle with the brush part tied around her tail until she could raise her calf. "Broomstick" cows were sold when their calves were weaned. Some ranchers would "sew" a Coke or a wine bottle inside the cow to hold the uterus in place. The cow would have died from infection and her calf would have starved if the rancher had not done something.

Now and then we would find an animal with a large abscess most likely caused by a cactus thorn. Cattle that needed to be treated would be driven to the house and held securely in a chute where the wound could be lanced with the point of a sharp pocketknife and the putrid yellow pus drained. Sheep were most often roped and doctored in the pasture. I always felt a sense of satisfaction knowing I had helped relieve the critter's pain and hoped the wound would soon heal. I also learned to splint a sheep's broken leg, draw medicine up into a syringe, and give injections. Dad would slap a horse's front shoulder a couple of times before inserting the sharp needle. They never even felt it.

Roswell Livestock Commission Co.

One of my first independent responsibilities after I could drive was to carry feed and water to a sick cow who was "down" out in the pasture to strengthen her in hopes she would recover. If they improved we would "tail" them up and drive them to the house to feed and doctor. Some died in spite of our efforts. We always felt badly when we lost a patient. Everything I had learned about caring for sick and injured animals proved invaluable to me in my later nursing career.

Nothing is more beautiful than a soft clean brown and white Hereford calf or a group of frisky white lambs playing chase. That alone made it worth all the work and worries. Sheep and cattle ranching in arid New Mexico was our life.

Not too baaad—one black, and one white lamb

When the work was done, ranchers could play. Sometimes they had dances in their homes or in the barn, if it had a smooth floor. We would leave our house soon after lunch, and sometimes stop by a dirt tank, if it had rained, to bathe in the cold rainwater. Mom and I would get in on one side and turned our backs while Dad got in. After a swim the breeze felt cold when we got out. One time we saw a rattlesnake rapidly swimming away from where we were splashing.

We dressed in our "party" clothes and drove on to the host ranch, where we had a covered-dish dinner before the dance. I was put to bed in the back seat of the car, and was only vaguely aware of being carried in and placed back into my own bed at home sometime after we got in around dawn. These were the only occasions I can remember my parents sleeping late.

Mama had helped me make a playhouse, using neatly cut firewood out at the woodpile behind the rock house. It had a little bedroom, a kitchen, and a living room with a fireplace at one end, all made out of sticks and logs. It had no roof. This is where I decided to play one morning while my folks were sleeping soundly after a dance.

Dad had emptied his pockets onto the dresser the night before. There was a pocketknife and a handful of change. I took it out and arranged it neatly on my make-believe fireplace mantel. What good was a fireplace without a fire? So, I went into the rock house and helped myself to a box of wooden matches. I soon had a fine little fire in my fireplace. Suddenly my whole woodpile house was in flames.

I ran to the house as fast as my small legs could carry me yelling, "Fire! Fire!" still clad only in my pajamas and little blue bunny slippers. On the way I stepped on a flat-headed roofing nail that went right through my slipper and foot, just missing the bones between my toes. My screams brought my parents running. Dad tried without success to save the woodpile while Mama pulled the nail from my injured foot and cleansed the wound with soap and water, painted it bright red-orange with Mercurochrome, and covered it with a Band-Aid.

Grandma Long said to soak it in warm water with Epsom salts in it several times a day, so I sat with my foot in a pan until Mama said I could get up and play. I have no idea whether we had tetanus shots back then. I do know Tom and I were never allowed around the barn without wearing shoes or boots. We found Dad's coins all melted together in the ashes. His pocketknife was ruined. No more playing with matches for me.

Sheep

When my father said, "We'd better sell that darn horse before it hurts someone," I wasn't one bit sad. In fact I was delighted. The big palomino he was pointing to had already ruined my summer.

My cousin, Marney, had come to help round up sheep one summer when we were teenagers. We had overslept, so we had to ride the only two horses that were left in the corral after the other riders had already disappeared from sight over the hill. We soon learned why the big palominos had been left behind. Neither gelding had been ridden much and were both still quite wild. "Hey, Marn, we'd better put them in the little corral. They'll be easier to handle there." We each roped and bridled one. Between the two of us, we managed to get them saddled and rode them around the small pen a few times just in case they wanted to pitch. It was much easier to stay on a bucking horse in the solid walled corral where the horse didn't have much room to get up speed and power.

We were almost to the back of the pasture and ready to start gathering sheep when the horse I was riding decided to throw me off. He did so without any warning. The world seemed a blur as I spun helplessly in the air. I landed on some of the sharpest, hardest rocks on top of one of the roughest hills for miles around. My clothes were almost torn off of me except my Levis and boots. I couldn't move one leg and thought it was broken. I could feel my ribs pop each time I sucked in a painful breath. I hurt something awful!

"Oh my gosh! Babs!" Marn shouted as she quickly climbed off her horse to come to me. "Are you all right?" It didn't take long for both of us to realize that I was badly injured. She took off her shirt to keep the hot June sun off of me until we finally decided she would have to ride back to the house to get help. She rode fast, but it still seemed forever before my folks came as near as they could get in the car to haul me to town. Big red ants crawled all over me and helped keep my mind off of the terrible pain while I lay motionless. Not a single one bit me. They were still crawling off of me in the car. A few even made it to the hospital.

A tall rigid nun from Saint Mary's Hospital's office came in to ask questions while I was lying on the hard x-ray table, still in severe pain. She sharply asked about my "accident." I told her, "It was no accident. That darned horse threw me off on purpose."

My leg was not broken, but my back and several ribs were. I spent several weeks in bed at home in town. Mama let me have their front bedroom where I could look out toward the street. My friend, Louise, brought me a yellow kitten. Mama tied a string on the end of a stick, so I could play with it on my bed. My neighbor, Kim, came to play Monopoly. She and I wrote each other IOU's when one of us was behind, and continued our game almost daily all summer.

Sometimes I sat on our front porch swing feeling sorry for myself while watching and listening to neighborhood children running and playing across the street. I really missed getting to swim when I saw them getting ready to go to the pool. The worst disappointment of all was knowing I had missed getting to attend my first New Mexico Military Institute Final Ball. I was devastated when I learned my date had taken someone else to the dance after I had been injured.

The sharp rocks had torn a golf ball size chunk of flesh from one hip. I suppose that was why my leg wouldn't move at first. The open wound had not been cleansed well in the hospital and would-n't heal. Thick green pus slowly soiled the gauze bandages my mother changed several times a day. There was the sickening odor of rotting flesh from which I couldn't escape. We tried all sorts of treatments recommended by the doctor, then tried Grandma Long's home remedies, which usually worked, but didn't this time. Alas, months later I still had a putrid seeping wound that my mother insisted I must show to almost all of her lady friends. "Barbara, show her your sore." Teenage girls DO NOT like to go around pulling their pants down.

Dr. Williams examined me again and again. He finally spoke to my mother, "I'm sorry to say this wound isn't healing. I'm going to have to order some sterile maggots to eat away the rotting tissue or else try acid to burn the bad part out in hopes it will heal. The only other thing would be to surgically remove the open area around it and that could leave her a lopsided bottom and possibly damage some of the nerves to her leg." He looked at me and said, "Young lady, I really don't want to have to cut on you."

I could picture the awful screw-worm maggots crawling in my body like they did in the animals, and immediately chose the acid. (I think it was carbolic acid.) I dropped my britches and bravely leaned across the treatment table with Mama firmly holding my arms and shoulders while the nurse passed a brown bottle to the doctor. He carefully poured liquid into the hole on my hip. It smoked. "Damn!" The only way to describe the intense pain is to compare it to the red-hot branding irons used to cauterize gun-shot wounds I'd seen being done in western

movies. I wished then that I had tried the maggots. It took me the rest of the long hot summer to recover.

Shearing in the early spring was one of our busiest times. We needed a lot of help, so Dad brought at least two hired men out from town. Special pens and chutes were put in place days before the roundup. A crew which had been contracted months ahead came in a caravan bringing their machines mounted on a long truck-bed so several men could be shearing at the same time.

Neighbors, their children who were old enough to ride, plus a hired hand if they had one, would either come the night before or drive for hours through the dark early morning. I hated getting up so early. Dad would call, "Rise and shine," after he and Mama had prepared breakfast. We were ready to saddle up and ride out as soon as it was light.

Part of the way out into the pasture Dad would instruct each

rider as to where he wanted him to go. "Ronald, you and Nabor take the north tank. Be sure to check back in the corner. I saw some sheep grazing there a day or two ago. Richard, you and Marlene ride over toward McKnight's pasture. Dick, go help Alton down the draw. Roy, ride up the west fence, then you can help Ronald. Barbara and I are going over around the north well." And off we rode with each rider turning toward their destination as we rode along side by side.

When I was ten and older, Dad would sometimes have me go with the riders while he stayed to direct the shearing of sheep we had rounded up the previous day. I never thought it strange that he had me tell my uncles and other grown men where each should go to gather the

stock. They never seemed to mind with the exception of one teenage boy who had been hired to help. He was sent back to town the next day.

The sheep were rounded up, one large pasture at a time. It took hours to ride to the far side, then to locate hundreds of the wooly animals which were spread out over thousands of acres. Many were out of sight shaded up under small bushes or hidden down in deep ravines. The ewes were gradually found grazing in small groups or walking along dusty trails headed to water. The main herd grew larger and larger as each rider added his small flock. They were then driven slowly to the house and penned in the corral.

Everyone helped move the sheep along into progressively smaller pens, so the shearers could easily catch a large wooly ewe or buck by the hind leg and pull it onto a wooden panel to keep the wool clean. The skilled shearing crew bent over each animal and gracefully guided the hand-held, motor-run clippers over the sheep so each long fleece of wool came off in one undamaged piece. It was then rolled into a soft bundle, tied with a paper cord, and tossed up into a large jute bag held upright on a rack where a man would stand on it and tromp it down so that more wool would fit into the bag.

The shearer took a flat metal washer and placed it on a wire hook near his shearing "drop" after he turned the naked sheep loose. That is how they knew how many sheep they had clipped at the end of each long hard day. Dad paid the *jefe* (the boss),  and he took care of his men. When we were young, they would put us down into an almost empty wool sack and let us hop around and play until it was nearly full and we could climb out. It was great fun, but I often got ticks in my ears.

"Mama, my ear hurts," I complained that night after being with the sheep all day.

"Go get the flashlight. I'll look." I thought she was going to pull my ear off while she lifted it first one way, then another to get the right angle to look down into it. "Yes, I see a tick. You lay right there until I get the oil." The warmed Singer sewing machine oil felt soothing when she slowly poured it into my ear. Soon I could feel and hear the large repulsive-looking blood-filled tick crawl out. She then either gently blew cigarette smoke into my ear or would make a "tea" from tobacco to pour in to stop the pain. It worked.

Dad would plan a short rest break after the stock was safely secured in the corral. Everyone came to the house to have a drink of cool rainwater pumped from the cistern. Mama would either have a snack or an early lunch if it was around eleven o'clock, since breakfast had been served around four or five o'clock that morning. Dad called out, "Barbara, run up to the house and see when Mama wants us to come in for dinner."

She always sent me back to say, "Fifteen minutes. Come in and wash up." That's how long it took for her rolls to bake.

Mom was a wonderful cook, which everyone appreciated. It was not uncommon to have twenty or more for lunch. They usually ate in the yard under the cool shade trees. Each one would bring his empty plate into the kitchen and thanked her for the delicious meal. The two large pans of hot rolls were always gone before the men went back to work. Dad thanked her also. Occasionally some of my aunts, Margaret, Syble, or Dorothy, would come to help with the cooking and doing dishes. They were all good cooks. Mama helped them at times, too. My mother would also work in the corrals when she wasn't cooking or cleaning up. A good ranch wife was half of the team.

After the sheep were shorn, they were all clean and bright white. They looked much smaller without their fluffy wool coats. A paint brand was placed on their side. T for Tom, my dad's nickname, was his sheep brand. Different colors were used for each pasture to help keep them identified in case the fence washed down or they found a gate carelessly left open by "town people."

Ranch sheep were shorn before they had their lambs in the early spring so they would seek shelter when it got cold; otherwise they would stand out in the cold wind, snow, or freezing rain covered with a thick fleece of wool, and let their almost naked new-born lambs freeze. When clipped, they would take their lambs to find shelter in a ravine or wherever they could be protected.

Also, a pregnant ewe heavy with wool would sometimes lie down and not be able to get back up. She and her unborn lamb would die unless the rancher happened to find her: another reason we rode around the ranch on a regular basis.

My favorite part of shearing was having the crew and their families stay for several days. They camped and cooked outdoors with their big black Dutch ovens over an open fire. The cooks made delicious pinto beans, roasted a mutton which Dad always furnished, and best of all, they made the most fantastic homemade flour tortillas I have ever eaten. They were not to be found at the grocery store back in those days.

I ate with the shearing crew almost every evening they were at our ranch, and always visited the cook when we went to help shear at neighboring ranches. Sometimes it would be a man, sometimes a woman, but they were always willing to share a tortilla. Some had children I could play with. One girl, a couple years older than I, carefully explained how babies were "made," by swimming with water bugs. No wonder she didn't know how to swim. I've often wondered how she learned the truth about babies.

Wool was a valuable crop until recent years when synthetics became readily available. Army and Navy winter uniforms and blankets were once all made from America's sheep clippings. Now that the demand has dropped, the price of the wonderful natural fiber will hardly pay the cost of shearing. I liked a bumper sticker I saw a few years ago to promote the sheep industry: "EAT LAMB - THOUSANDS OF COYOTES CAN'T BE WRONG."

Marking lambs was another busy time when folks came to help. Rounding up sheep with young babies was slow tedious work since we had to be careful not to lose any of the tiny ones too young

to keep up with their mothers. Sometimes the ewe would have "hidden" her baby under a bush or beside a rock and we would have to search until we found it. Carrying two or three newborn lambs on the front of the saddle by the time we arrived at the house was not unusual.

My, there was a lot of noise while we had them penned in the corral with all the lambs and ewes calling for each other, "baa-baa, maa-maa," hour after hour. It was a pleasure to watch as a mother and her baby finally recognized each other. The ewe would sniff the lamb skeptically as it was doing its best to nurse. When she was finally satisfied it was hers, she would stand still and its little tail would wag with joy. There were usually a few who failed to get back together; we raised these dogies on a bottle. They became pets.

The best pet I ever had was a dogie lamb named Whitey. She would follow me anywhere. We won a blue ribbon at the Halloween parade as *Mary Had a Little Lamb*. Dad used her for a lead sheep when she was grown. The gentle ewe would bring her twin lambs to the house and would paw on our backyard gate to ring the bell on it until someone would let her into the yard to graze or to feed her some dry bread.

Once in the corral, the lambs were separated from the others and herded into a small catch-pen. The "catchers" grabbed hold of a baby, held it securely with all four legs facing forward, then crossed one

Grandpa Corn

front and one rear leg to hold them in place with their left hand and the other side with their right. The sheep's head rested against the holder's neck, with its tail pointed toward the "marker" on the opposite side of a waist-high platform where the small animals could be supported firmly on the bench. Children were always eager to help mark as soon as they could catch and lift the smallest ones. Older kids gradually worked their way up to the larger lambs. There were always a few that were too heavy or had such sharp horns it took an adult to lift and hold them.

The markers, usually Dad and my uncles, stood across the counter prepared to vaccinate, dock the tail, and clip each lamb's ears in a pattern designated by the Livestock Board when the sheep brand had been issued as legal proof of ownership. Bucks were castrated and became wethers. When I was young, castration and tail cutting was done with a sharp knife; later on, a thick rubber band called an "elastator" was used to cut off blood circulation. The dried parts would fall off several weeks later. This was much less traumatic for the animals.

Last of all, a paint brand was carefully applied to the lamb's side. My mother often did this job. They were then gently placed over the fence and out of the holding pen to return to the corral full of continuously bleating ewes. Several hopeful mothers would run to inspect and sniff each bewildered baby as it returned to the flock. They were all soon happily reunited and turned back out on the range to graze. This process was repeated for each of the three pastures at our home, the Rock House Ranch, and later at our Brown Lake Ranch about ten miles further west. If more than a few sheep had been missed when we marked or sheared, we had to round up all over again.

The last major sheep roundup of the year was in the fall when they were gathered to wean the almost grown babies. Most of them were nearly as large as their mothers. Some of the ewe lambs were saved for breeding stock. The wethers would be sold to be fattened for slaughter.

Ewes with no lambs or little prospect of raising one, were culled out to be sold. We checked their teeth. There was no need keeping one that could not chew. A long blue chalk mark was put down the back of the "dry," "broken mouth," or "spoiled bag" old "Nellie" ewes to be hauled away with the freshly-weaned lambs. Long trucks would come to haul them away in double-deck trailers. Dad would use Whitey to help load them. My brother Tom has always said, "Cattle for pride, sheep for profit," since they produced wool as well as meat.

Sometimes sheep had to be "drenched" to kill internal parasites that would slowly sap the animal's strength away. The animals were all funneled into a narrow chute that was about waist- high to my father. He and one of my uncles would work their way through a dozen or so sheep at a time, holding each one's head firmly, tip it upward, and place a six inch long stainless steel tube into their mouth and squirt a grape juice-colored vermicide down their

throat. The ewes were a comical sight as they would lick their lips and shake their heads afterward. The flock would slowly gain weight and return to good health.

When I was fifteen I had a bad accident while we were marking lambs, which brought me nearer to death than any other time in my life. Dad had a fifty-five-gallon drum of gasoline on the back of the truck in which he had hauled it from town. He called out, "Barbara, go fill the pickup so you can drive over to the south well to see if we missed any sheep."

"Sure, Dad." I was always thrilled at the chance to drive. I was to take a hose and siphon fuel from the barrel into the pickup. I had done this with water before, and had watched my father suck on the gasoline hose to make it flow. Just as I was beginning my second hard suck, gasoline suddenly flowed into my mouth and lungs before I knew what was happening.

Dad heard me coughing, spitting, and cussing and came running. He helped me into the house where I got out of my gasoline-

soaked clothes and washed myself. My lungs burned something fierce. Mama said, "Get into bed. I'll take you to town as soon as I finish these rolls." I could hardly breathe. She quickly finished in the kitchen then rushed me to town and called the doctor. Reassured, my mother left me at Grandma Long's house, thinking I would be all right. She needed to get back to the ranch to feed the roundup crew.

My fever shot up, I had chills, and my chest finally got so painful Grandma called Doctor Williams, who came to the house to see me. By that time, it was all I could do to breathe. I had chemical pneumonia and was so ill I don't know how I got to the hospital. Thank goodness for penicillin. It saved my life, even though I had a sore bottom from getting shots every four hours around the clock for several days. I was on oxygen and had a hot rubber mask on my face attached to the tall green tank at the head of my bed.

My folks came to town when they got word I was so sick. They bought a fan to cool me off and to try to blow the terrible gasoline odor out the open window since the hospital was not air-conditioned. I coughed up that awful taste for weeks, and have hated the smell since then. Dad came in one day after he had finished shearing. He blinked back tears as he told me my pet ewe, Whitey, had died. I cried and cried.

The nuns at Saint Mary's were good to me. They remembered me from the summer before when I had been thrown from a horse. I'm sure my accident was often repeated to others as a lesson to never siphon gasoline.

The June 29, 1950, Saint Mary's Hospital bill for several days:

Room	40.00
X-ray	10.00
Penicillin Injections	3.00
Other Medications (oxygen)	1.65
Tax	1.50
TOTAL BILL	**$56.15**

When I was very young we had a large pet lead sheep that had been raised by my mother's father, Grandpa Long, on a bottle as a dogie lamb. Dad used him to guide the other sheep into the pen. Gabriel, a castrated buck, had grown a fine set of curled horns and knew no fear. I once bent over to pick up a small ball, and he ran and butted me in the rear. I was more frightened than injured, but always looked to be sure he was not near when I left the yard. Gabriel certainly was no angel in my book.

Cattle

The winter I was eighteen months old, I was standing too near the long feed trough across from where my father had been feeding some cattle. I just happened to be in the wrong place when a cow with long sharp horns suddenly raised her head and caught me in my open mouth. The horn didn't even cause a scratch on my lips or face, but hooked upward into my upper palate, pushing my two front baby teeth up into my nose.

My poor terrified parents rushed me to town some twenty miles from their Eden Valley house to the dentist in Roswell. He removed the two teeth and reshaped the roof of my mouth as best he could. One other front tooth was loose and turned crooked. I remember being called, "snaggle tooth" by some of my uncles and still cringe anytime I hear a child called a name referring to their looks or unfortunate circumstances. Mama said I didn't even cry in Doctor Connor's office chair, but looked up and simply said, "Light." Looking back, I am surprised there was no infection. There was a great deal of concern at the time that the "seed" teeth had been destroyed. Again, I was fortunate to get a good set of perma-nent teeth before I started to school. They came in with saw-like ridges on them, but I had them smoothed off when I was a teenager. I learned you should never stand too near an animal with sharp horns. Dad sawed the sharp tips off all the cows' horns and dehorned young calves after this accident.

My father and I were riding along a broad green plain one day when we spotted a tiny newborn calf lying sound asleep in the tall grass. We were only a few feet from the well-concealed baby when we saw it. Dad signaled for me to stop and to be quiet. He then motioned for me to get down from my horse as he was doing. The mother cow had gone to water and was safely out of sight.

We slowly bent over the beautiful creature and gently ran our hands across its dark reddish-brown back. The fine wavy hair felt like silk. The calf opened its large brown eyes and looked up at us through long curled lashes. It showed no fear. I felt its curly snow white face, looked at the soft pink nose, and the long, hair-covered ears. I couldn't resist touching my face to the perfect little head. It finally stood upon unsteady long legs and watched us slowly ride away. Dad hadn't said a word.

Quite often one cow would stay with several young calves and "baby sit" while the rest of the mothers went to water. Sometimes the "sitter" would be a young heifer, the cattle version of a teenager. Nursing calves don't have to have water every day, but the cows do.

Branding was necessary to prove ownership in case stock got through a fence onto the wrong ranch, or were rustled. Cattle cannot be sold in New Mexico without one. It is much more than just a mark placed on livestock. Most ranches are recognized by their brands. Many are used for generations. My father's **IHI** brand had been registered to legally identify his cattle and horses since he was a young man. He also used **T** to mark his sheep. They later went with the ranch when my brother, Tom bought it. We never branded our horses. Dad thought it cruel and unnecessary.

Branding calves and dehorning was another busy time on the ranch. The rounding-up process was basically the same as with sheep, though cattle always seemed easier. There were not as many, and they were usually more willing to go where you wanted them to rather than run and scatter as sheep were prone to do. Once they were penned, the calves were separated from the cows. This was difficult, since neither wanted to be away from the other.

Once in the pen, they were large and often dangerous. I would hear someone shout, "Look out!" and then I'd turn and see a grown man making a mad dash and a heroic leap up and over the high corral fence to escape a snorting frothy-mouthed charging cow. Many a brave soul has had to run or hurriedly scramble over the fence to get away from an upset cow. An angry cow with a young calf could be a much greater threat than our large Hereford bulls with their wide set of horns. The bulls had weights placed on their horns when they were calves in order to train them downward so they would be less likely to hook and injure someone or another animal.

When I was young, we had to gather firewood and build a hot fire to heat the metal branding irons so they would scar the calves' thick hide. The air was full of the acrid smell of burning hair. Later on a butane burner was used to heat the irons. The introduction of

such modern improvements as the "elastator" for castration, and eliminating a wood fire to brand with, ended the era of roasting "mountain oysters" over the branding fire.

At one time calves had to be roped and held on the ground for branding, which was hard on man and beast alike. Dad bought a metal squeeze chute in which the calf was clamped securely, then rolled to one side to lay it down at table height so each person could work on it at the same time. Each was branded, earmarked, and dehorned; all were vaccinated and tick medicine was placed in their ears. Bull calves were also castrated.

The table was then tipped back upright and the befuddled calf was ready to return to the comfort of its mother's udder. All of the cattle were sprayed to keep flies off, then released back into the pasture. A few workers could now do as much in a short time as it had once taken several men a long hard day to accomplish.

One day, while we were separating the cows from their calves in the corral, Uncle Richard started jumping up and down, stomping his feet, swearing, and pulling down his britches all at the same time. He had been standing in a large bed of very angry red ants. Dad and the rest of his brothers roared with laughter. Richard didn't.

Another thing that helped make our work easier as the years went by was Dad's constant improvement by breeding better and more placid stock. He always sold wild-natured animals. Most of their stock was so gentle he and Mama could round them up by themselves by the time they retired. They had moved to the Brown Lake Ranch where the terrain was much less rough and rocky after they sold the Rock House Ranch to my brother.

My mother drove the pickup slowly to the house, while my father teased the animals with a little feed from the back of the pickup as the sheep or cattle slowly followed my parents into the corral. Dad would place a bale of alfalfa hay just inside the gate where the sheep or cattle in front could see it and would step inside the solid walls of the corral. The rest followed. The saying goes, "Don't work harder, work smarter."

It certainly was an improvement over the earlier days I could remember when Grandpa Corn still owned Brown Lake and there was not even a cross fence to help funnel his wild cattle into the corral. Dad, his five brothers, and their hired hands would spend the best part of the day rounding up and driving the large herd to the stock pens. By that time the men and horses were tired and tempers were short. That's when the real problems began. Some wild-eyed cow would nearly always get spooked as it neared the corral gate. She would bolt and take off toward the lake in a cloud of dust, with one or two of the cowboys riding hell-bent to turn her back before the rest of the herd decided to follow. Sometimes they would. It would then take another hour to get them back and ready to pen all over again. I heard words my mother told me I was never to repeat.

Once the gate was closed behind the last straggling calf, the men came to the house to get a drink of cool rain water. Everything was fine. One of the Corn "boys" would say to Grandpa, "Pa, you'd best sell that darned old cow 'cause the next time she runs off I swear, I'm going to shoot her." My grandfather never said a word.

Cattle were rounded up again in the fall and went through much the same process as the sheep to separate out what would be

sold. When I was young, cattle and sheep were hauled to the Santa Fe railroad stock-pens in Roswell and shipped to Kansas City by train. Dad and one of his brothers rode in the caboose to make sure the animals were periodically unloaded, fed, and watered properly. Later on, stock could be trucked to a sales ring in Clovis. My uncle, Thoras Dye, finally built a livestock sales barn in Roswell, where one of my LAZY-A-BAR cows was the first to be sold.

Selling stock in the fall was the first income we had since contracting our wool in the spring. A good lamb and calf crop depended on whether we had enough rain to grow first-rate pasture grass to fatten the animals. Getting a good market price was also very important. Paying off notes owed for money loaned by the bank to buy the ranch, rendering government grazing fees, taxes, living and operating expenses, and buying breeding stock all depended on these animals.

There were no built-in "benefits" such as health care and retirement funds for ranchers. They had to save for their own future. Mom and Dad were conservative with money. We had few frills when I was young, but never lacked for anything we really needed. I suppose going through the Depression made an impression on my parents. Tom and I both learned to be frugal.

I had grown up watching my parents writing checks to pay bills or to get cash. By the time I was a freshman in high school my heart was set on having my own checking account. I approached my folks with the idea after I had sold a couple of steers that fall. My check was for around $300, a fortune to me. After I brought the subject up I was pleasantly surprised when Dad said, "That sounds like a good idea," and took me to the bank a few days later. He stood by while I opened an account and left with my very own book of blank checks. I felt rich. Back at home my father showed me how to record the checks I had written and to subtract them from

the balance. Wow! I was ready to roll.

I went to town, the last of the big spenders. Christmas shopping without having to ask for money was a dream come true. I gave Tommy a metal Firestone auto station, complete with a working elevator and gas pumps that filled small cars with water. I  bought sodas at Platt Drug after school for my friends. An afternoon cherry lime root beer float became a necessity. My mother looked and listened as I explained my numerous purchases. She never once asked a price or showed any disapproval. My checks were never for more than twenty dollars, but that would buy a lot back then. Some were for only a dollar, but I had gone through page after page in my check book.

One night after the supper dishes had been done, Dad told me to bring my bank statements and check book to the table. "It looks like you're about out of money," he exclaimed as he inspected my records. I hadn't worried. I still had a good supply of blank checks. My father sounded concerned, "You mean you've already spent all of your cow money! What do you plan to do now?"

"Well, I guess I need some more money," I replied not having a clue where it would come from. We carefully went over each of my extravagant expenditures one by one. This was much worse than having to ask my parents for money.

At long last, he stated, "I'll give you $200 and that will have to last you until..." Dad gave me some date that seemed to be forever. From that time on I've had very few problems staying within my means. I had learned a valuable lesson. It took more than a book of blank checks to be wealthy.

Cattle and horses stood around all day in the summer trying

to swat flies with their tails. In fact, they could hardly graze with the hordes of flies biting them and getting into their eyes. The flies infested even the smallest sore until it was a major wound, then hatched their vicious flesh-eating maggots. DDT powder came along and saved the day. We had seen it being dusted on war refugees to rid them of lice and other external parasites as we watched the newsreels at the movies.

We sprayed our cattle every time we gathered them, with a homemade sprayer that Dad had fashioned out of a heavy-duty oil drum. It was powered by removing a spark-plug from the pickup engine, then screwing a gadget back into the hole with an air hose attached to pressurize the barrel from the top. DDT, which had been diluted in water, was sprayed through yet another hose with a nozzle out of the bottom of the horizontal barrel. At times we hauled it out in the pasture to spray a few cattle at a time.

Our kitchen screen at the ranch would get black with flies, especially in the late summer when it began cooling off and they wanted to get into the nice warm house. "Barbara, get the swatter." Mama kept me busy killing and sweeping up the pesky insects. They really liked to sit on the warm linoleum where the sun shone in through the east kitchen window in the mornings. Sometimes I could swat two or three with one swift swing of the wire mesh flyswatter which always hung on a nail behind the kitchen door.

Mama closed up the doors and windows so Dad could also spray the back porch. It was a wonderful relief until some of the flies built up immunity and the insecticide had to be made stronger and stronger.

The incidence of plague, which is endemic in New Mexico, went down while DDT was being used since it also killed the fleas that transmit the disease. It was later learned that DDT had possible cancer-causing properties in mice when they ate a lot of it, so was taken from the market. Other less harmful products have since replaced it, but it was truly a miracle chemical in its day. The flies were never quite as bad again.

We always had one or two milk cows. I learned to milk at an early age and was good at it. I had to milk fast before the cow could eat all the "sweetfeed" I had poured into her trough which my father had fashioned out of an old hot-water heater. Being occupied while eating was the only way she would stand still. At first I felt as though my tired hands would fall off squeezing and pulling on the long teats, but my fingers soon grew strong. Mama always said I brought more cream to the house than Dad. I think he would get tired and let the calf have it.

"Barbara, why don't you milk tonight. I'll help Mama with the dishes." Dad's offer was music to my ears. I really disliked doing dishes, especially having to be so careful with the fragile gallon glass milk jars. The hardest part was scalding all of the dishes plus the stainless steel milk bucket and strainer with boiling hot water from the two large teakettles on the stove.

My folks took care of the milk once I got it to the house. It was strained and refrigerated right away. The next day Mama skimmed the thick yellow cream off. Some was used on cereal or for cooking. We made the rest into butter in the square glass Daisy churn. The soft yellow clump was placed in a cereal bowl, the top patted smooth with a wooden paddle that Dad had carved from a shingle, and my mother's unique designs marked across the surface.

Sometimes it was a flower, their IHI brand, or my LAZY-A-BAR if I had helped turn the handle long enough. We shared our milk, butter, and eggs with Grandma Long.

The milk-pen

calf always became our beef since the cow was either a Jersey or a Guernsey bred to one of our Hereford bulls. Cattle buyers "docked" the price of any mixed breed or mismarked calves such as a "line-back" or a "red-neck." They said they wanted them to all look uniform in the feed lot. We always suspected it was really the buyers' subtle way of taking advantage of the ranchers. The calves we raised at the house were always better fed and fatter anyhow.

Dad later began to "cross-breed" his cattle after Tom studied agriculture at New Mexico State University and Texas Tech University. He added some Black Angus bulls to the herd. Cattle buyers had finally learned that the most important thing was meat production, not the color of the cow. Profit rather than beauty was the business approach to ranching. My father gradually changed with the times.

I made a pet out of a handsome young Hereford steer calf Dad had bought to raise on the milk cow, since she had much more milk than we or her own calf needed. His name was Lazy Bones. He would come up to me in the pasture. I could even ride him. When he was almost grown, I hooked the large steer up to my brother Tom's new wooden wagon with the bright red side-boards, thinking he would pull the cart. He did. Away he, the wagon, and my little brother went. All was well until Lazy Bones cut the corner around a big feed trough and a front wheel hit it. The wagon stopped but Tom did not. He wasn't badly injured but his beautiful new toy was ruined. I was in big trouble. Dad had planned on butchering the steer when large enough, but he was too much of a pet to eat, so he eventually had to go to the sales ring. Never name an animal you intend to eat.

Coyotes & Other Critters

When I was young it was the custom to hang dead coyotes on posts along the highway that passed through Eden Valley between Roswell and Santa Fe. Some said it was so the despised varmints would see their dead relatives and be afraid to cross the road into sheep country. I'm surprised they gave the mangy critters credit for that much intelligence. Whatever the reason, there was more than half a mile of fence along the road with at least one dried carcass tied to each post.

I was with my parents early one frosty winter morning as they were driving across some of our relatively gentle rolling hills when Mama suddenly spotted a large flock of sheep gathered in a closely packed herd, slowly milling around and around. "Irwin, get the gun! There's a coyote in the sheep. Hurry!"

They both quickly sprang into action. Dad handed Mom the old Winchester 30-30. "Barbara, hold on tight!" So, off we went, bouncing across the prairie.

There was not only one coyote, but two. One had jumped upon the back of a ewe that was trapped inside the tightly packed flock. He was trying to get a death grip on the poor, defenseless sheep's throat. In the meantime its wily accomplice was stealthily working its way along the outer perimeter of the panicked herd in order to grab hold of a leg or flank with its sharp, yellow canine teeth. Both were so intent on their prospective kills, they hadn't noticed our old, black Ford approaching.

Mama took aim on the outer critter. Dad said, "Don't shoot yet, Bertha! You'll hit the sheep." About that time the sheep had seen us and began to break away from the panicked herd. The outer coyote saw our car and turned to run to safety. Too late. CRACK! It dropped dead in its tracks. The sharp report of the rifle had caused the other malicious varmint to release its tight hold on the ewe's throat and escape in a frightened run.

Dad drove over to look at the lifeless hairy body of the coyote my mother had just shot. As we got out of our car Mama said, "Don't touch it. They have fleas." She held my hand as we slowly walked over to it, still a little hesitant about it really being dead.

The coyote almost looked like it was still running as it lay there on the ground. Its yellow-gray winter fur coat was flecked with a few dark hairs. The long, bushy black-tipped tail was sticking straight out behind. I had seen smaller versions of fox tails tied to automobile radio antennas in town. "Can I have the tail?" I pleaded.

My request was met with a scowl. "No!" was my mother's sharp reply. "You can't have that disgusting thing."

I squatted down in front of the dead animal and looked, fascinated by its dark eyes, already glazed over in death. Its wide mouth seemed to be fixed in a ghastly smile. "Look, he still has wool in his teeth."

"Don't touch it!" I was reminded. "Now, Barbara Ann, get away from that awful animal," Mama sharply commanded.

Dad nudged the limp carcass over with the pointed toe of his boot. "It's a male," he remarked, "We'd better get a coyote chase together right away to get the other one. It's probably this one's mate and she may have a den full of pups."

My concerned parents scanned the grassy area looking to see how much more damage the devious pair of predators might have caused. "Look! There's another one down," Dad called out to my mother as he pointed to a wooly gray body lying on the ground, almost hidden by the tall dry grass. His careful examination revealed that the young ewe, heavy with her unborn lamb, had her throat viciously torn open. Damp, red blood was still slowly oozing from the ugly wound. She had probably been dead for less than an hour.

I'd been wandering around the area while Dad was bent over inspecting the dead sheep. "Mama, here's another one!" I shouted as I walked over to the still body which was already cold and stiff.

"Those darn coyotes must have been in the sheep all night," my upset father declared angrily.

By then Mama had walked in the opposite direction. "Quick, here's one that's still alive." Sure enough, the poor mother sheep, lying helplessly on her side, was still kicking and trying her best to get up from the cold ground, which was covered with bits of wool that had been ripped from her tender hide. No blood was visible, but it was obvious she was badly injured. When Dad turned her over we could see that her flank had been brutally torn away to completely reveal her damp, silver blue stomach and snake-like small intestines now falling from her opened belly. My father pointed to a small white membrane pouch inside the almost gutted animal. It contained a tiny lifeless unborn lamb.

"Bertha, go get the gun. I'll have to put her down." I could tell my father and mother were both sad. I looked away and cried.

By the time we were through searching, we had discovered five dead or dying prime young ewes, some of the best of our herd, needlessly destroyed. Those two coyotes had not killed for food alone; they had murdered for sport. All of the dead ewes were to have lambed in the early spring. It was especially heartbreaking to see how much pain they had suffered needlessly. Their deaths also represented a direct loss of income and untold damage to our long term breeding program. A very distressing day indeed.

Most of the ranch country around the Pecos Valley where my great-grandfather and his sons had pastured their stock had been open range with few fences. Their cattle had grazed from the Pecos

River to the foothills of the Capitan Mountains, covering almost 300 square miles. Ranchers from all around gathered them in the spring, separated their stock to brand, then rounded them up again in the fall to sell as mature fat calves. This was still the custom when my father was a young man, but barbed wire fences were being used to keep cattle in place by the time my parents bought the Rock House Ranch.

Sheep were still under herders, however, and could walk under the lower wire of the two-strand barbed wire cattle fences. There were no barriers for coyotes, bobcats, and other small animals. The diligent sheepherder, with a flock of up to a thousand animals to look after, was the only protection the sheep had from predators.

My parents started building sheep-proof fences soon after they bought the ranch. All of the livestock could now spread out and graze without needing to be under herd. Other ranchers were doing the same. Their goal was to cut down the death loss due to the unwelcome varmints and to better utilize the grazing land. Ranchers were trying to make a living while wool, sheep, and cattle prices were at an all time low during the Depression. The early years of my childhood seemed like an open war on coyotes.

Government and privately paid trappers were enlisted to help catch eagles, bobcats, and coyotes. Mexican eagles came to feed on newborn lambs in the early spring. These huge, strong birds could lift and fly off with a newborn lamb or goat. Coyotes and bobcats fed on sheep and young calves year round. None of these predators were protected at the time. Bobcat pelts could be sold; there had once been a bounty on coyotes.

The trappers were a colorful lot. They came with their bedroll and a flask bottle of "scent" carefully wrapped in cloth and tied to their saddle. It held the secret to their success, a vile mixture of collected coyote and bobcat urine and musk guaranteed to attract varmints into carefully concealed traps. These unique men fascinated me, but they smelled horrible. I hated to sit near them when they ate with us.

I'd missed the end-of-school picnic in the first grade because

I had chickenpox. I was broken-hearted. My parents felt sorry for me. Mama was busy with infant Tommy, so Dad and I took many a simple picnic lunch when we rode out in the pasture to help make up for my disappointment. One day we went to check traps which he had set to try to catch a bobcat that had been killing sheep. We were almost under some large shade trees near a water hole in the creek bed when we heard the simultaneous frightening sounds of a wildcat's growl, limbs breaking, and chains rattling above our heads. Our frightened horses almost jumped out from under us. The large predator had pulled the trap up the tree with him and was not happy.

"Here, Barbara, hold my horse." He pointed with one hand and held his old 30-30 carbine in the other. I led our horses away from the noise and Dad shot the hissing bobcat entrapped in the knurled old hackberry tree and left it there to rot. I could hardly wait to get home and tell Mama. The now quiet water hole made the perfect site for our picnic that day.

One of a rancher's regular responsibilities was to "ride the fence" to watch for places where coyotes had dug under the net-wire to pass from one pasture to another. We were able to drive our car across some of our ranch boundary, but the more rough and rugged north pasture had to be patrolled mostly on horseback.

When freshly dug holes and coyote tracks were identified, ranchers would organize a chase by designating a time and place for their friends and neighbors to meet. They came just before dawn to ride horseback or drive slowly across one pasture at a time in as near a straight line as possible in hopes of "jumping" and shooting one. Riders would go where cars or pickup trucks could not.

When a coyote did jump and run from its hiding place, those nearest would speed recklessly after it, trying to dodge rocks, mesquite bushes, and ravines while pulling out an old 30-30 carbine or a shotgun to attempt to shoot the fast-moving target. Dad would drive as fast as the rough terrain would allow. Mama would throw one leg over me to hold me safely in our pre-seatbelt car while she was shooting out the window trying to kill the despised critter. "Irwin, turn left. I can't see anything but the car hood. You'll have to drive so I can see to shoot." My mother had the reputation of being an exceptionally good shot.

When I was older, I roped an almost exhausted coyote that had been cornered by a fence before anyone else arrived to shoot it. I was more than a little pleased with my daring accomplishment. My cousin, Harold Corn, embellished the tale and told it around school in his deep voice which closely imitated his father Lee's curb-side story telling style. "Hey, you boys better get Babs to give you riding and roping lessons. Hell, she rode right up and roped a coyote while all the rest of you guys were just lolly-gagging around." It got more colorful and exaggerated with each telling.

I was mostly embarrassed, but a little pleased by his praise. All of my boy cousins and their pals included me anytime I wanted to join them. Dad did draw the line and responded with a very definite "No!" when they wanted me to go to the mountains and camp out with them to go deer hunting.

I usually rode our horse, Dixie, on coyote chases since he had a nice comfortable rolling trot that was wonderful when I was in the saddle all day long. He was our best all-around horse. Years later when the sorrel grew old, stiff, and in pain with arthritis, Dad had to put him down. My father later remarked, "Shooting Dixie was about the hardest thing I ever had to do."

I never carried a weapon, even though I was quite a good shot with a rifle. Dad didn't own a pistol. When I asked why we didn't have one he replied, "Well, I figure they are a lot more dangerous to have around children, since kids like to play with them. Besides, it's a lot easier to hit something with rifles or a shotgun." Guns were simply considered necessary tools on ranches.

Airplanes were sometimes used to hunt in later years with some success, but it seemed that no matter how many coyotes were killed, more always made their way up from the Pecos River to the east. They multiplied there, thriving on jackrabbits before moving west into sheep country where they were not welcome. Their numbers gradually decreased as the years went by. At least the net-wire fences helped slow them down.

Large mule deer and graceful pronghorn antelope gradually began to appear as the coyote population decreased. None had ever been sighted on our ranch, and were rarely reported in any of my uncles' pastures when I was young. Before I graduated from high school, only one small herd of antelope lived on a ranch between our place and the Capitan Mountains. They pretty well stayed inside fenced pastures while deer gracefully hopped right over the five-foot tall obstacles with little effort. Foxes also made an appearance after most of the coyotes were gone.

Now and then we would see a porcupine. They mostly stayed down around the draw where they had small walnut, hackberry, willow trees, and bushes to live in and eat the tender bark. Sometimes we would find a curious young lamb or calf with quills in its face. They would starve if we didn't find them to pull the spines out, since their mothers surely wouldn't let them get to the milk supply with the sharp, three-inch black and white needle-like barbs in their nose. Horses and cattle would occasionally get the quills in their lower legs. Sores would fester and run until the quills had been removed. Some of the animals seemed to appreciate our help; most did not.

One time our collie, Susie, attacked a porcupine while following me on a ride in the pasture. She was on top of the bristling animal before I even saw it. There was no calling her off once she had started her attack. The dog let out a painful yelp as she tried to get the sharp quills from her face with her paws. That didn't help, since they have a tiny barb at the end; it takes a firm pull to get them out.

I dismounted and managed to get most of them out with my fingers, but Dad had to use the pliers on some of them. They were even in her mouth and throat. We ended up taking the poor, suffering dog to town to the vet to remove the remaining quills, since she had to be anesthetized to get to them. Susie left porcupines alone after that painful lesson. The same was true of her one and only encounter with a skunk.

Getting to ride out over the hills was a wonderful way to observe nature. We were granted the privilege of seeing animals being born— and sometimes dying. I had just topped a ridge on my horse one day when I saw a large hawk swoop down and grab up an unsuspecting helpless cottontail rabbit. It let out one pitiful cry. Its limp lifeless body was soon carried off to a twig nest of baby hawks for their next meal.

One of the most beautiful sights at the ranch was watching a mother quail bring her nest of dainty young birds into our yard to stand, drink, and take a shower from the lawn sprinkler. They all scurried along behind her in a neat miniature parade. All of the wildlife has benefited from the improved water supply provided by the wells drilled and maintained by ranchers.

Tiny

"Mama!" I cried out after I found myself lying on the hard ground just beyond the open kitchen door. I was sobbing and gasping for air since the fall from my Shetland pony had painfully knocked the wind out of my four-year-old lungs. "Tiny threw me off again."

"Well, you'll just have to get back on," she replied.

"Oh, do I really have to?"

"Yes," she said in a matter of fact tone as she came out, dried away my tears, dusted my clothes, and sat me back up on the small saddle. "If you don't, he'll keep on bucking. Hold on to the horn and show him who's boss this time."

Tiny had been a surprise. My folks had stopped at a large white frame house out east of Roswell on the Berrendo Draw one afternoon as we were on our way to the ranch. I had to stay in the car with Mama while Dad went inside to talk to a man. They were soon loading a small, black horse into the homemade two-wheel trailer we were pulling behind our nineteen-thirty-something tan Chevy. It was a beautiful small Shetland pony named Tiny, and he was mine. I was excited to have a horse of my own.

The long road to the ranch seemed to never end. It was dark when we got to our first pasture. The road from town was a mere thirty-five miles or so, but the last thirteen was only a rocky trail of parallel ruts made by covered wagons, later to be followed by automobiles. There were five gates to open, drive through, then close. The drive took a little over an hour in good weather but was often impassable when wet. It was beginning to rain; Dad stopped and let Tiny out into the wet, dark open range so we could hurry on to the house before the road got too bad. I cried, feeling sorry for my pony and myself.

Tiny was the most ornery and contrary critter I have ever known, but I loved him dearly. He surely knew how to pitch, and bucked me off almost daily when I first got on. I soon learned to lead him inside the yard where dirt had been hauled in to plant a Bermuda grass lawn. It made a much softer landing spot. I shed many a tear in pain, and more in frustration, with that stubborn little pony.

Sometimes Dad would make a rope rig for Tiny to pull my little red wagon, but his laid-back ears put us on notice that he didn't like being a draft animal. No self-respecting ranch horse would.

That fall we brought horses to town to ride in the colorful Old Timers' Fair Parade. There were fancy decorated floats, a band with prancing majorettes, and way too many horseback riders to count. I won a prize for being the youngest rider. The large Corn family always had a float covered with dozens of joyful whooping and hollering cousins, aunts, and uncles, many whom I had never seen before. A wide banner on each side of the float said, "Corn Crop—19___." Dad's colorful Aunt May always seemed to be in charge of the fun-loving bunch. Dad often said, "I'd much rather have her for me than against me." She was always one of my favorites.

As I grew older and became a more accomplished rider, I was able to saddle and ride Tiny without help from an adult. This is when the real test of wills between the ornery little horse and me began. He would fill his belly with air before I tightened the cinch so the saddle later became loose. Once it rolled off his back and almost under him with me on it. At least he stopped and didn't step on me or run and drag me over the rocks and cacti.

One of his favorite tricks was to use his head to lift the metal hook out of the gate latch to let himself and any other animals in the corral escape. Dad would come to the house, visibly upset, and say, "Barbara, you forgot to lock the gate again and all of the horses got out."

"I closed it. I know I did," I protested. "Nabor must have left it open." There was usually only me to catch the blame until one day Dad finally caught Tiny in the act. He then felt badly about having scolded me.

Another bad habit Tiny had was to turn his head and bite me on the rump just as I had my left foot up in the stirrup, ready to mount. That really hurt my backside as well as my pride. He even bit Dad once as he was tightening the cinch. Boy, was he angry!

Tiny did a good job keeping up with the large horses. Once, when Dad and I were riding across country to a neighbor's ranch almost ten miles away, his horse was trotting at an easy pace and Tiny, with his short legs, had to lope to keep up. All of a sudden I heard the unforgettable nerve-chilling buzz of a rattlesnake under my horse.

Tiny jumped up and over it, carrying us both to safety. It was fortunate that I managed to stay in the saddle. Dad dismounted, killed the snake, and petted Tiny with affection. He said nothing to me at the time, but later was overheard bragging to the neighbor, "If Barbara hadn't been such a good rider she would have fallen right on top of that big rattler." What my father had said made me

feel really good inside. It was a number of years before he mentioned the incident to my mother. She still became upset, knowing I could have been killed.

The last time I remember riding Tiny was one morning after a hard rain when the Rock House Draw in front of our house had run and filled all of the small water holes. I thought it would be fun to ride through one, and had no problem urging Tiny into it where the water came just above his knees. He then surprised me by starting to lie down. I quickly got my feet out of the stirrups and jumped into the water before he got all the way down. My new boots were filled with water and mud. I was a little frightened and very angry as I led him back to the house.

Tiny got sick and died the year I started to school. I still remember how long and soft his winter coat would get and how I used to comb and brush him. The whole family was sad when he died. He had been my first animal friend.

Other Horses

We had a herd of mares when I was young, but they were too wild to handle. Dad sold them and bought geldings for our ranch work. Most of my uncles raised horses, so we had an ample supply to choose from for replacements. Dad bought a good-looking bay quarter horse at the sale in town when I was a teenager. He was busy putting horseshoes on it when I arrived at the corral. "What's his name?" I asked. Just then the horse kicked.

Dad shouted, "Dammit!" So that's what always appeared on the program when I later rode him in horse shows.

One of my most embarrassing moments came when I was riding Dammit in a horse show at the New Mexico Military Institute polo field. We had lined up with the other riders on their mounts as directed by the judge. Some fancy eastern horse breeds are trained to stretch out with their two front legs spread away from their back legs. This really looks sharp. My shiny bay decided to take this position just as the judge was coming our way. Colonel Norton looked up at me with an approving look and smiled, silently complimenting my horsemanship skills.

"Oh, shoot!" I thought. I knew exactly why my horse had extended his stance. He let his water go in a fierce splash of strong-smelling yellow foam which splattered up on the judge's freshly pressed trousers as he was standing next to me, pinning a ribbon on Dammit's bridle. Several of my less than bashful male cousins let out whoops of laughter and called my name, "Hey, Babs, I'll bet you can't do that again." I just wanted to crawl in a hole and hide on the NMMI polo field that day.

Mama and both of my grandmothers always seemed to come up with a true-to-life example of what might happen if you did or didn't do the right thing in order to prevent accidents. I expect I've done that myself. My mother referred to an event which happened when I was very young to illustrate the oft-repeated lesson to never trust even the gentlest of horses. It seems Dad had put me up in the saddle of a very tame horse tied to a post so Mama could take my picture with her Kodak when I was about a year and a half old. Something startled the old black gelding, and he jumped to one side. I fell off onto the hard ground right on my head. There were no long-lasting injuries since my little straw hat had helped protect me, but I have often wondered if that bump on the head was why I've always had so much trouble with math and spelling.

After Tiny died, I advanced to full sized horses. They were taller and harder to saddle and bridle, so I'd need to have Dad or a hired man help me. I usually rode Mama's gentle horse, Midget. I either used a five-gallon feed bucket from the barn or climbed up on rocks, fences, or whatever was handy to help me reach the stirrup to get on my horse.

Dad finally gave me a fast, black gelding named Polecat with a white star on his head. He was smaller than Midget. I soon grew tall enough to be able to saddle him and mount without help, a great feat of independence for me since I could now ride whenever I wished.

Pole Cat could outrun all of our other horses. In fact, he really liked to run. I fancied myself a jockey, cropped his mane short, and was about to start cutting his long, black tail so he would look like the race horses in the movies when Dad intervened. I was really in trouble when my folks learned I had sawed the leather-covered wooden horn off of my small Shetland saddle so I could lean over Pole Cat's neck like the Kentucky Derby riders did.

I tried to race anyone who was willing. My cousin Marlene was the only one who was interested. "I'll bet Pole Cat can outrun your horse, Sox," I challenged.

"No way," Marlene replied confidently. "Just meet me over by the south well and we'll have a race."

I nodded my agreement. "How about day after tomorrow around ten."

So, we met to have our big match. We carefully drew starting and finish lines in the dust across a smooth stretch of graded road, then lined up side by side. At the count of three we were off. Each of us gave it our best, leaning forward in our saddles and encouraging our horses to run faster and faster.  Marlene started to take the lead but I urged Pole Cat on until we were a nose ahead.

"Come on Sox," Marlene shouted excitedly as the powdery tan dust was flying behind both of our mounts. Our great race ended in a tie. We were both champions. Now we were ready to take on all comers, but unfortunately had no challengers. She and I never raced each other again. I think both of us were afraid we might not win a second time.

One day a brief afternoon thunder-shower came. There was a perfect bright rainbow across the draw in the east. I had been waiting for an opportunity to get to chase one and look for the "pot of gold" I had heard stories about. I could see exactly where one end of this rainbow was, near a large boulder not far from our house, so I quickly ran to the corral, saddled Pole Cat, and took off to find the treasure. The rainbow moved away as I rode toward it, first one way, then another. It and my childish hopes soon faded to end another fantasy.

During the war years we had a big mean bay horse named Hitler; another one was called Mussolini, a fast little sorrel; and Tojo, who was so mean he was sold for dog food. Mickey Mouse was a long-legged, dark gray gelding that Dad liked to ride. He was so tall it was

Mom and Dad

hard for me to mount, so I rarely rode him. Tommy and I both had palominos when we were older.

Mama rode with Dad and me before I started to school. She was a good rider. We rode around the ranch checking salt troughs near watering places, and looked to see how the stock was doing. Dad knew each animal and understood more about livestock than I would ever know. He could look at a cow and quote her genealogy and calving history backward and forward.

I was often frustrated by his instructions, "Go get that cow. No! Not that one. The broomstick cow's calf." I was bewildered and so was my horse. They all looked alike to me. His voice would get louder and louder until he was shouting. "Come on over here and mind the gate. I'll just have to do it myself." And he did.

Once my father and I were both riding horses that were still on the wild side, or "rough broke." We rode to the north tank where we saw two badgers running from the water. Dad was afraid they would dig holes, which could easily break a horse's or cow's leg if they stepped into one.

He started running his horse over one of the badgers in hopes his horse would kick the badger and kill it. His horse thought otherwise. It started to pitch just like a rodeo bronc. Dad just about had the horse settled down when it took a big jump and tossed him off into a prickly pear cactus right on the seat of his pants.

I rode off to catch Dad's horse because it would be several miles across rugged country for him to have to walk back to the house. My father was busy pulling out the painful thorns, and yelled, "Tie those horses up and come help me get these durn stickers out of my legs." He hollered again when I did, and said he'd rather do it himself. He had to stand up in the stirrups all the way home because he was still full of small spines that he couldn't get out. We never disturbed the badgers again.

Several years before, one of the few times I didn't go riding with Dad, he came limping into the yard all dirty, leading a badly injured horse named Pinto Pete. Pete, with Dad on him, had stepped in a badger hole and fallen on a sharp rock, tearing a triangle-shaped piece of skin on his front shoulder. It was wider and longer than Mama's hand. She and I were busy sewing it up when Uncle Thoras happened by and helped us. When we were through doctoring the horse, we took Dad to town. Dr. Williams said he had a broken collarbone and several fractured ribs. My father and the horse both made a full recovery.

Pinto Pete was a good horse. I taught him to rear up like Roy Rogers' horse, Trigger, when I lifted the reins straight up. He would stop, or "whoa" when you pulled the reins back toward the saddle horn. Aunt Arline's "greenhorn" husband, Paul, was riding Pinto Pete one day and asked, "How do I stop?"

I said, "Just pull up." The horse stopped and then reared. My

uncle was surprised, but so pleased with the praise he got for being a "real cowboy" that he wasn't upset with me.

Dad was! "He could have fallen off and been hurt," my father sharply scolded.

Tom learned to ride on Pinto Pete when he was young. One time during a round-up, the colorful black, brown, and white-spotted horse came walking slowly up to the house before the rest of the riders were back with the herd. My little brother was sound asleep, holding on to the saddle horn. The gentle old horse stood quietly at the gate until Mama took the small, sleeping boy off and led the horse back to the corral. Tom had many other horses when he was older, but now ranches with two-wheelers. The horses were all retired from ranch work and just put out to pasture. "Collecting Social Security," Dad called it.

I spent a lot of time with the horses when I didn't have anything else to do. I loved to ride out in the pasture. We kids especially enjoyed making our horses jump over the spiny yucca plants, which often grew several in a straight row, creating a perfect obstacle course. We first started with the low ones and progressively advanced, urging our horses over much taller ones. I pictured myself riding in the Grand National Steeplechase along with Elizabeth Taylor in the movie, *National Velvet*.

My cousins, Marney and Marlene, were my favorite riding companions. We all shared the same love for horses when we were young. All three of us were very accomplished riders since we had been raised on horses. Marn made a career of teaching riding. Marlene and I usually helped each other when we were rounding up, so we often rode together.

Uncle Ronald always had a large herd of horses, and once picked albinos out of his herd for both Marlene and me. We later rode them as matched pairs in horse shows when we were in high school. I named my horse Blanco and trained him myself; he was the best horse I ever owned. I was especially proud of the fact that I had taught him to come to me in the pasture when I whistled.

As I grew older I was allowed to ride my horse to neighboring ranches all alone. Marlene and I would meet at our south well to swim, or I would occasionally ride Blanco over to spend a couple of days with her. One day I rode north to visit my friend Marianne at their ranch. It was a long day's ride there and back, but it felt good getting to ride alone across the vast expanse of grass land spotted with yucca and mesquite bushes. The only sounds I could hear were my horse's steady footsteps, his steel horseshoes clicking against an occasional rock, and the distant shrill call of a hawk circling in search of a meal. Mrs. McKnight had a nice lunch for us, and we girls chatted about our summer vacation and the coming school year. I had a long ride home so I soon walked out to their corral, saddled my now rested and fed horse, and was on my way. I stopped and went skinny dipping at our north well on my way home. My only instructions had been, "Be home before dark." I was.

My father had driven around every watering place in our Bajillo pasture the previous week. He had counted all of the young, bred heifers over and over. Finally at the supper table one evening he declared, "Some of our cattle are missing. Barbara and I are going to ride down the draw to see if they could have gotten into the north pasture."

We saddled up right after breakfast the next morning. Mama

handed Dad a bag with two Peter Pan peanut butter sandwiches. "Here, you may need these." My father always carried a canteen of cool cistern water on his saddle in the hot summertime. There wasn't much conversation when riding with Dad. He would occasionally point out a small herd of sheep quietly grazing on the side of a rocky hill, "Look, there's that ewe with the black and white twins." Sure enough, one was coal black and the other snow white. Most of the time we rode along together in comfortable silence.

We rode through every small bunch of cattle we came across looking for the missing heifers while following the fence line between pastures, always inspecting to see that the wires were intact. We finally came to the back of our property. Dad dismounted and unwired an old gate into the neighbors' pasture. Again we rode along miles and miles of fence line. Each time we saw some cattle we would slowly turn and ride among them, looking for my father's IHI brand. We rode on all day, pasture after pasture, until we were finally down to the highway at Eden Valley.

My father pointed and said, "When I was a boy there used to be a flowing spring over where you see those bushes. We called it Antelope Spring. It's been dry since the drought during the Dust Bowl," he went on. "Sand and dirt would blow in from Texas and Oklahoma in a huge black cloud. It got so dark our chickens went in to roost. It hasn't rained as much since then. The government never should have had those people plow up so much of the country for homesteads. Most of it's just too dry to farm."

My mother's greatly appreciated peanut butter sandwiches had long since been digested by the time we returned to our house late that evening shortly before dark. Mama met us at the kitchen door when she heard the yard gate bell jingle. "Where have you two been? Are you all right? I've been worried. I'll warm your supper. Go wash up." She hadn't given either of us a chance to say a word. Dad filled her in on our long day's events after supper. I bathed and went right to bed. We never discovered what had become of our heifers.

I was only slightly involved in riding in our local Pecos Valley Horsemen-sponsored horse shows. I much preferred riding at the ranch to going around in circles at the whim of the judges. Blanco discovered the bright red Coca-Cola stand where bottles of soda had been placed in coarsely crushed ice. He loved to eat the cold chunks. He once pulled loose from where I had him tied. It didn't take me long to find him back at the Coke booth, where he had attracted quite a large crowd of admirers who were busy feeding him ice. I've never known of another horse that liked it.

Blanco also loved being sprayed with a water hose during the hot summer, and would strain his neck around to get just the right spot wet. I rode him bareback in dirt tanks. He especially enjoyed swimming. Sometimes I would just hold on to his tail and let him pull me around. I had to be careful when he got out though because he would lie down in the dust and roll while he was still wet and turn his gleaming white coat into a mud ball. That called for another swim.

Another embarrassing time for me was at a junior rodeo held at the Chaves County Sheriff's Posse rodeo arena, which my parents had helped build when they were members. I was suddenly handed the American flag to carry as I rode in the grand entry parade at a high run. Dammit was a fine horse at the ranch, but he never really got used to the noise and commotion of city events.

That darned horse bucked, jumped, reared, and tried every trick he knew to try to get rid of me and that flag all the way around the large arena. I was still holding on to the banner, which was becoming terribly heavy waving in the breeze at our buck-and-run gait. Finally some gallant cowboy rode up alongside me and took the flag. The crowd roared with shouts of approval. That was Dammit's last trip to town.

Chaves County Sheriff's Posse

Dad and I rode across our house pasture on an extremely cold and windy weekend day, most likely in January. We were looking for a bull that my father wanted to drive back to the corral, to be fed to improve its stamina for the breeding season. We had ridden most of the way to the back side of the large expanse of grassland with the freezing north wind cutting right through my clothes. My legs, face, and hands were numb. I had a wool jacket and a head scarf, but the cotton Levis and leather gloves I was wearing were hardly any protection against the miserable chill.

My father said, "You go on up the draw toward the 3-C tank to look for the bull while I ride on over the hill." I kept on moving, but slowly. My horse Blanco was no more eager than I was to be out in the ice cold wind that felt as though it surely must have blown all the way from the North Pole. Finally, I was near enough to see that there were no cattle. Dad was not in sight, so I decided to dismount and take shelter from the sharp wind in a shallow gully where I could curl against the dirt wall. It seemed to be getting colder by the minute. I had a firm hold on my horse's reins as I huddled, trying to get warm.

It seemed only seconds before I drifted into a sound, peaceful sleep, and no longer felt the cold. I don't know how long it had been when Blanco tugged against the bridle and woke me. I just wanted to sleep. He kept waking me off and on until Dad finally rode up and saw I was in danger of freezing. We forgot about the bull and rode back to the welcome warm shelter of home. Mama made me a hot toddy with sugar and whiskey and sent me to bed to get warmed up. I think I would have frozen if Blanco hadn't been there to wake me up, and for my dad to be able to see and therefore find me.

I spent many happy hours with our horses, first Tiny, then all the others. They were not only necessary for doing ranch work, but riding was also my favorite pastime. They were my companions when I was young. I talked to them and knew they understood. At least they were safe to share my most intimate secrets with. They also helped me vent a lot of teenage energy and frustrations while riding over the rocky hills or down a freshly graded road at full speed with my short blond hair flying in the wind.

My favorite place to ride was to the top of a high hill where I could see almost forever. My eyes swept the pure horizon from the red bluffs of the distant Pecos River in the east to the prominent blue silhouette of the Capitan Mountains in the west, listening to the peaceful silence of the wide-open space, and feeling close to God.

Windmills

Dad and Uncle Richard decided to drill a well near the fence-line between our ranch and theirs. Finding a reputable driller, then waiting for him to bring his ancient up-and-down-style drilling rig was a frustrating affair. They had already waited a year to get the steel pipe and sucker-rods because of war shortages. When the driller finally got his primitive rig all set up, we were eager to see the water flow, but progress was slow. Water for the men and machines had to be hauled in over the rough ranch roads. Cables would break; the helper would quit, or get drunk, and thrown in jail until someone went to town to bail him out; the well driller's wife's relatives came to visit; the list of delays went on and on.

The noisy diesel engine chugged night and day turning steel cables which in turn lifted the heavy metal "digging" tool up and down in the ever-deepening hole, grinding away eons of hard gray limestone an inch at a time. It took months, but the well was finally completed. The next step was to erect a steel windmill tower, place the heavy bladed wheel on top, and construct a large metal water storage tank.

I had been at Girl Scout camp while the tower was erected,

and was anxious to see how it looked when I got home. I saddled
Blanco to ride over and see it before the mill was assembled on top
of the small platform on the tall steel structure. I tied my horse to
a cedar fence post and climbed up the narrow metal steps until I
reached the top. There I sat on a four-foot wide platform that surrounded a large open center where the water pipes and pumping
rods would later pass up through the center of the mill.

I slowly stood and marveled at the magnificent view. I felt like
a bird up in the clear air with nothing but sky above and around
me. At first I felt like holding my arms out and sailing like the
graceful black vultures soaring in the distance. I truly had a birds-
eye view from atop the tall tower.

My joy was short-lived. It almost turned to panic when I suddenly realized I was getting dizzy. The small cottony clouds that
had been slowly moving across the azure blue summer sky now
seemed to be stationary, and the once steady ground below was
now rotating around and around. Oh my! I immediately sat down
where I had been standing on the narrow metal rail and tightly
gripped the edge with white knuckles, waiting for the world to stop
spinning. I thought, "There is no way I am going to be able to climb
back down." I just clung on to the cold metal in desperation until
I finally focused on Blanco waiting patiently below. I realized I had
no choice but to make my way back down the ladder, so I slowly
descended step by step, looking only at my hands until I reached
the ground. My legs still felt like jelly as I mounted to ride home.

I was back in school when another crew came to erect the
mill, which had to be pulled up in pieces with cables, then bolted
together. Dad came to town as soon as this job was completed and
the bladed wheel was ready to be turned into the wind to pump the
precious water from the depths of the earth.

I had rarely seen my father angry, but he was when he got to
town that day. He told of how one of the pilots from the air base in
Roswell had spotted the men working on top of the windmill and
found great sport in buzzing the tower. The pilot flew around and
around getting closer with each roaring pass.

The men on top were clinging to ropes and steel, hanging on
for dear life. Dad could see they were terrified and in danger of

falling to their death, so he pulled his old 30-30 rifle out of the worn leather scabbard in the pickup and waved it in the air as the young daredevil pilot made another pass. Thank goodness, he understood the message and flew away.

A well almost 600 feet deep, powered by a large twenty-foot Samson windmill on a tall wooden tower, pumped a small stream of cool water into a large rock water storage tank at our house. It had been built in 1915 when Grandpa Corn had the well drilled. Livestock on open range, and later held in fenced pastures, grazed on around twenty thousand acres. They all watered at the Rock House Well. Years later a smaller Aermotor mill replaced the huge old Samson atop the tower.

At times stock water was supplemented by rainfall and runoff caught in man-made dirt tanks, small usually dry lake beds, and a few natural water holes in the arid hilly pasture land. When there was neither wind to turn the mill nor rain, there was a serious water shortage; times were tough. One hot dry summer Dad had to borrow Grandpa Corn's pickup to haul water from Uncle Ronald's Deep Well Ranch because our windmill was broken. Our animals had to have water.

When I was older the wide smooth top of our rock tank at the house made a great place to sunbathe after a swim, and to watch lace-winged dragonflies, or the small hawks we called "bull-bats" skim gracefully across the water to drink and scoop up insects floating on the water. I often just sat there and daydreamed while watching the feathery clouds change from one imaginary form into something else, while the black turkey buzzards soared almost effortlessly above on the summer up-drafts.

My least favorite ranch task was working on windmills. It was usually either a terribly hot, or even worse, a cold, miserable, and dusty day. Dad always did the work on the high platform near the top and sometimes had a hired man helping below the tower. Mama drove the car slowly backward and forward, pulling the cable through the pulley. This raised and lowered more than five hundred feet of sucker-rods from the well, one section at a time, so the valve at the bottom could be serviced every few months.

It took all day to pull the well when everything went as planned, with only a short break for lunch. "Barbara, go in and check the beans," Mama instructed. "Add a little water from the teakettle if they are getting dry. Oh, go ahead and put the salt pork in. It looks like we can eat in about an hour." Lunch wasn't fancy when my mother had to drive. She kept Tommy safely in the seat beside her when he was small.

The driver had to stay alert and watch for Dad's slight nod up or down in order to keep a steady pull to prevent breaking a cable or a rod, which could be life-threatening to those near the well, or at least extremely expensive to repair. He would shout, "Barbara, hurry up, bring me the grab wrench," or some other tool. Once I was standing too near the cable as it swished by my upturned face and slightly chipped a tooth. I was lucky it didn't get my face.

It was an even harder job when the pipes holding the rods had to be pulled after the sucker-rods had been removed. A truck was needed to lift this heavy load. It took at least two days plus often a long trip to town for parts. It was essential to get the mill back into action as soon as possible to replenish the water supply for our stock and all of the wildlife that depended on it.

Sometimes there wouldn't be sufficient wind to turn the mill enough to water all of the stock, so Dad would hook a big gasoline engine up to a pump-jack in order to make it pump water. It was a dangerous set-up, with a long drive belt that could easily pull an arm into the tight gears and chew it off. I was forbidden to get near when it was running.

Later, Dad bought a set of long steel rollers to back the car up on to make the rear wheel turn the pump. It would run for hours until the gas tank ran dry, then he would go fill the Ford with gasoline to keep it going all day and night. Running out of water was the worst thing that could happen on a ranch. We were always careful not to waste water. We eventually had three more wells drilled so stock wouldn't have to walk so far. It was an expensive, but worthwhile, improvement.

We used our windmill tower at the house to hang up a fat calf or lamb to be butchered. Sometimes we had a pig or two to be killed in cold weather. Slaughtering pigs for pork was a lot more work than skinning a beef or mutton. Barrels of hot water had to be heated and the hog dipped down into it to loosen up the stiff bristles. These could then be scraped off with the edge of a large kitchen knife, much like shaving them. Dad was skilled at butchering and was always very particular and clean with our meat.

My father once saved a pig bladder, washed it out, and pumped it full of air to show how he and his brothers had made their own footballs when they were young. Mama thought it was repulsive and soon did away with it.

We always shared our meat with our grandparents and Dad's brothers, and they shared with us. This was especially important before we had frozen food storage. I always looked forward to eating fresh heart, liver, brains, and sweetbreads when we butchered.

Grandma Corn made spicy hogshead cheese, and Grandma Long prepared wonderful chewy pickled pig's feet. Sometimes the hired men would skin and roast the sheep's head. They offered me the eyeballs but I never accepted this delicacy. They looked much too gross.

Our house well was so deep that a nice cool breeze came out of the big ten-inch pipe casing around the well. I would feel it and listen to the strange noises it made. Uncle Ronald told me it was the

Chinese talking on the other side of the world, and I could get there if I dug a hole deep enough. I spent many an hour trying. When visiting China as an adult, I asked a young Chinese lady where their children were told they would arrive if they dug a hole deep enough to get to the other side of the world. She replied with a smile, "Australia."

It was relaxing to lie in bed at night and listen to the slow, gentle, monotonous squeak, squeak, squeak of the windmill turning. Every windmill had its own special sound. The next thing I knew, it would be morning.

Brown Lake Ranch

The Brown Lake corrals were the most uniquely colorful pens I have ever seen. They were mostly built from salvaged deserted "squatter" houses that had been abandoned when the Dust Bowl drought starved the homesteaders out. Along the corral walls you could see where each door and window had once been.

Grandma Corn once explained what a hard time those people had, and how the present day Brown Lake chicken house had once been someone's small home. How sad life must have been for the few brave souls who eagerly came west for free or cheap land, to later painfully learn that it was just too dry to raise crops in this desert country without irrigation, and impossible to support a family on as little as 640 acres. Some had left their hopes and homes behind without even taking the dishes from the table.

Grandpa Corn's Brown Lake Ranch was several miles west of our Rock House Ranch. It provided an awesome view of the rugged east end of the majestic Capitan Mountains, which was made even more prominent on the landscape by the gentle slope of the surrounding countryside. On clear days it looked as though you could almost reach out and touch the beautiful blue El Capitan mountain.

Several shallow dry lakebeds with hard cracked earth and a few hardy weeds eagerly awaited a summer thunderstorm to make them bloom and free the multitude of toads entrapped in the hard earth below. There was a quiet charm to the wide open countryside.

I don't know just how large the Brown Lake Ranch was when Grandpa bought it, but it was much larger than the Rock House Ranch. The most unique building at Brown Lake was the *chosa*, which is a house that's half dug-out and half above-ground. The word is Spanish, which more literally translated means shack, but we never thought of it as a "shack." It had been built near the usually dry lake bed long before Grandpa had bought the ranch,

The Chosa

so who knows when? Billy the Kid could easily have visited it on his trips between Lincoln and Fort Sumner.

The top part was built of local rocks put together with straw and mud, much like the one at the Rock House Ranch. It was in danger of falling down several years ago, when my father had men take a few stones out at a time and replace them with cement inserted until it had been restored to preserve its historical significance. The one-room building had a small wood-stove for cooking and heating. It had a loft for sleeping, plus one bed downstairs. It was warm during the winter and cool in the summer time.

The story was told of a woman going mad and hanging herself on the bare rafters; I don't know if that is true. I do know that rattlesnakes liked to live there. One once crawled out from beneath the old wooden steps just as my father stepped down. He was still partially blinded from going from the bright sunlight into the much

darker building and didn't see it. He narrowly missed being struck by the large upset rattler and was then trapped by it, tightly coiled and buzzing angrily between him and the only way out of the small dimly lit building. For all Dad knew, there could have been more than one snake down there. His voice still sounded nervous with fear as he often retold of this terrifying experience. We were always reminded to be cautious before going down the steps.

Ora Blanchard told my mother of a time she and her new husband were going to their ranch on the north side of the Capitan Mountains soon after they married. "We were caught by an unexpected late spring blizzard near Brown Lake and stayed out the storm in the chosa. We would have frozen to death if we hadn't had its shelter. First, we used up everything in the woodpile, and then even had to burn the furniture after all of the other wood was gone to keep from freezing." They later replaced it and the food they had eaten, as was the custom.

Grandpa Corn had a shotgun-type house built so he and Grandma would have a place to stay other than the chosa when they came to Brown Lake. He had a hired man named Pee Wee, who helped with the construction. It was built like a barn, with each wall put together on the ground, then raised and joined at the corners. There were no studs. It had two bedrooms, a very large kitchen and sitting room, as well as a nice long screened-in porch. There was no bathroom since there was no running water. We had to make do with a "one-holer" out back.

My cousin, Marlene, and I once turned the wooden latch on the outside of the privy door to trap a hired man inside. His urgent cries not only brought him help, but also got us in trouble. Dad and Uncle Richard later laughed at our prank when they didn't know we were listening. Grandma told my cousin and me how her "boys" had once turned the outhouse over with a man inside.

Grandma Corn came out to stay for a few days at a time. She

gave the house a woman's touch with curtains in the bedrooms. There was an old calendar with a photo of Will Rogers and Wiley Post standing beside the airplane they later died in. It hung in the kitchen for years. Blocks of ice were still used in an old icebox for many years before co-op electricity finally came to Brown Lake.

The chosa and the first corrals had been built near the lakebed long before a well was drilled a mile or two from the house. Who knows why it was drilled so far  away? Grandpa used a closed metal tank to store rainwater off the new tin roof for the house. My father had water piped from the well to the house and corrals years later when he and my mother moved into a mobile home nearby after they had sold the lower ranch to my brother Tom.

Grandpa Corn did not dehorn his cattle, thinking they needed their long, sharp horns to fight off predators. One of the first things my father and his brothers did after my grandfather died was to saw the tips of the cows' horns off. There was one wild bull Dad said they had never been able to get penned in the corral. It most likely died of old age.

The ranch was divided up after Grandpa died, with each of his six sons getting a pasture. Dad inherited the one with the east half of the lake and the chosa on it. He later bought the pasture with the other half of the lake from one of his brothers. Together the two large pastures make up the present-day Brown Lake Ranch. Tom bought this ranch when my parents retired in 1980. Mama was seventy and Dad was seventy-three.

I once learned a painful lesson at Brown Lake. Marlene,

Marilyn, and I could hear some strange sounds coming from the rusty old corrugated roof on the saddle house. "Let's get up there and see what that is," I suggested. We three curious girls rolled a couple empty fuel barrels over so we could stand on them to investigate. Something was moving inside the tiny holes between the ridged corrugated metal where it had been nailed to a wooden base. We soon found a loose corner. We all three pulled on it and raised it slightly to get a much better look.

There were several startled, small squeaking creatures under the tin. "Here, I want one," Marn called out as she reached out her hand.

"Me too," Marlene shouted in excitement as we all three bravely grabbed one up by its legs. They looked like rats with wings.

I had once seen a dead critter like this that had drowned in our rock tank at the house. I thought it was a bird but Dad had told me what it was. "It's a bat! Wow! Now we have some live ones." I was beside myself with excitement.

Marlene said, "I'm going to take mine home for a pet." Marney and I both thought that was a grand idea.

About that time, mine raised its ugly little head and sunk its razor sharp teeth into my finger. "Ouch!" I cried, as I immediately dropped my prize, "That hurt!" The bats were definitely not going home with us. We never messed with them again.

I had my first driving experience when I was five. My cousin Marney and I were at Grandpa Corn's Brown Lake Ranch with our fathers and uncles working stock. All the men were busy with the animals. Marn and I went up to Grandpa and asked, "Can we drive your pickup?" He probably nodded his consent, so we took off in his nineteen-thirty something Ford with a crank-out windshield for air conditioning.

We were both too small to sit on the low seat and still be able to see out the window, so we took turns. One of us stood on the seat and shifted the gear stick on the floor and steered, while the other sat on the floor to work the starter, gas, brake, and clutch pedals: true teamwork.

The Capitan Mountains

Somehow we managed to drive at least two miles across wide open country without a road, while skillfully dodging mesquite bushes and large rocks. We made it to the windmill and back without any major mishaps to the pickup or ourselves. It was years later before I wondered why Grandpa had let two five-year-old girls drive, or why our fathers had failed to intercede to stop us.

The Long Family

My mother, Bertha Long Corn, was tall and straight. Her regal walk and determined bearing left no doubt about her self-confidence and natural leadership ability. She always kept her short, light brown hair done up neatly with a beauty shop permanent, and carefully attended to her facial makeup and clothing even if she was only going out to the corrals. Her soft, green eyes sparkled when she broke into a full genuine laugh. She was attractive but never realized it.

Mama's love of nature was reflected in her beautiful rock garden and flower beds in town as well as her never-ending interest in every detail along the path, as we often went for long walks at the ranch or in the mountains. She loved all creatures, with the exception of snakes and a few people. We had lengthy talks as she explained and reasoned out the details of almost any topic that came into her head. History and geography became wonderful adventures in her frequent storytelling. My mother was sweet and loving most of the time, but could also be stern and strict. When she said "No," she meant it. Mama had just what it took to be a good ranch wife: self-reliance, initiative, and imagination. She was

well organized and always busy.

Mama was born and raised on a large cattle ranch in Lincoln County. Her father had worked there until they moved to Roswell, where she went to school. She was fifth from the eldest of eleven children.

My early years visiting at my Long grandparents' house were pure bliss. Mama's youngest brother, Pat, was only six when I was born so there were still "kids" at Grandpa and Grandma Long's house when I came along. I was not the oldest grandchild but the only one who lived nearby, so I was the recipient of much too much attention from the aunts and uncles who were still living at home in their large, white frame house on East Seventh Street next to the railroad track. I loved every minute of it.

Their house was in a quiet neighborhood. There were only two other small houses and the coal yard across the street. A huge, vacant lot joined their yard. Colorful wildflowers grew there. I once picked a handful and took them to my grandmother who thanked me graciously, placed them in a small jelly glass, and put them on the dining room table. Mama called them weeds and said they smelled bad, but Grandma liked them. The front lawn was hardy Bermuda grass, with large lilac bushes along the south side of the house. Oh, how sweet the violet blossoms smelled when they bloomed in the spring. A tall, wooden fence draped with trumpet vines stood guard between the house and the railroad yard.

Beyond the fence was forbidden territory. My Uncle Ray showed me how to look through cracks between the boards to see the trains. I liked it best when one would come up the siding right next to the fence and let out a jet of steam so close I could almost feel it. The huge steel wheels would slide to a stop, making the cars behind jerk and clank.

The giant black engine would huff and puff clouds of black smoke while the railroad workers ran up and down, disconnecting and rearranging box cars as we watched in fascination. Once while I was peeking to watch, Grandpa picked me up and walked to the end of the wall, so we could see everything from a grown-up's view. The engineer waved to us. Grandma soon appeared in her apron to call us in to lunch to end the great train watch.

Some of the vacant space in the massive railroad yard was utilized to make adobe bricks. Clay-like soil was mixed with water; straw was added a little at a time. Men would stir this brown muddy mess together with large hoes, then scoop up the thick dirty mixture with buckets or shovels and pour it into large wooden molds where it was dried in the sun. The frames were removed several days later and the handmade bricks stacked in neat diagonal walls to complete the "cure." A good "dobe" building, as they were called, could last hundreds of years in the arid climate.

My grandparents' backyard was large, probably not as large as it seemed from a child's perspective, but it held a barn, a saddle house, two corrals, a large metal tank for rainwater, and several double-deck rabbit hutches. The most unusual feature in their yard was a small outdoor building with a real flush commode that was to be used by "men only." I was told at an early age that ladies, and that meant me, went into the house to go to the bathroom. I didn't mind because it smelled better inside anyway.

Grandpa had a milk cow and a lot of rabbits that he butchered and sold to local housewives and meat markets. He dried the pelts and sold them also. My uncles, Pat and Ray, raised pigeons on top of their barn. Grandma cooked the young adult birds she called squab. Those and fried rabbit were extra-special meals for me.

The barn was always dark and interesting. I climbed on the hay and admired all of the interesting old relics stored there, such as a pair of ice skates which belonged to one of my aunts, a sled, and a number of moth-eaten old dry animal pelts my uncles had preserved. Several barn cats came around when Grandpa poured them a dish of warm milk before he took the bucket into the house. They helped keep the mice away.

I barely remember my great-grandmother Piersol, who died shortly before I turned four. She and Grandma Long sometimes sat in the backyard together on rustic grapevine chairs and a settee. My aunts told me to be quiet and very good the day she died. She had been a true pioneer woman on her early mountain homestead, but was a sophisticated member of the Shakespeare Club in Roswell before she died.

Grandma Long told of how she and her mother had nursed their badly injured milk cow back to health after it had escaped from the corral and been hit by a train. The Jersey they had when I came along was one of her calves. It had Grandpa's ZOE brand across her side, derived from his sister's name. (I learned most of the alphabet from brands.) My folks retired the old cow to the ranch when large animals were excluded from city limits.

Grandpa Long

Grandpa Long's family had moved from Maryland in the 1700's, living in Kentucky, Illinois, and finally Iowa, where he was born. He had come to Jicarilla, New Mexico, on horseback in 1888, near the gold boom town of White Oaks. My grandpa, Joel Long, had a combination saloon and store when he met my grandmother. He gave up his business after they married, thinking a bar was not a suitable place for a family man.

Grandpa then became a deputy sheriff in Lincoln County for several years, and also worked on ranches in the area until they moved to Roswell. They lived in the Chaves County Courthouse where he was the custodian. He also served as a part time deputy for ten years before retiring. The family then moved to the house on

Seventh Street. The courthouse closed for his funeral when he died in 1944.

Grandpa Long was very tall, and was bald except for a white fringe of hair around the back of his head. He usually wore bib overalls. He always came into the house and sat in his large easy chair to listen to the noon news before lunch. I was not allowed to touch the tall brown radio with the green eye that lit up when it was turned on.

Sometimes Grandpa would lift me up to his lap and let me help him stuff tobacco into his old black pipe, but I had to be very quiet when the news began. My fondest memory of

Grandpa & Grandma Long

my grandfather was when he would take me to see the rabbits. The white ones with pink eyes were my favorites. He had to move the mother and her tiny naked pink babies to a safe warm nest away from the other bunnies as soon as they were born to protect them from the papa rabbit.

Grandma Long's family were early pioneers in the Boston area, where they had come from England in 1632. Her branch kept moving west. My grandmother, Agatha Viola Long, was born in Iowa. Her father moved them to Texas, where he died when she was fifteen. Grandma married and had a baby when she was young. She divorced, then came to New Mexico, with her infant son, mother, sister, an uncle and her sister's fiancée in two covered wagons from Archer City, Texas.

Grandma was barely eighteen when they left Texas, on the twentieth of June, 1901, and arrived in Roswell exactly one month later. (It is now an easy six-hour trip by car.) I can only imagine how hot and difficult it was to travel back then. Grandma worked at White Oaks in a boarding house until she met and married my grandfather. They lived on ranches and her mother's log cabin homestead on the north side of the Capitan Mountains until they moved to Roswell.

Grandma Long was short and soft. She had long dark hair, which she let down at night, brushed, and braided before going to bed in her long flannel nightgown after she put her false teeth into a cup of water on the nightstand. She wore a whale-bone corset that had to be unlaced at bed-time. I often slept with her

The Long family

after Grandpa died. My grandmother always took time to give me a hug or to doctor my skinned up knees with red "monkey blood," Mercurochrome, which didn't burn. She used iodine when I got ringworm from the cats. She circled the reddened area with a ring of medicine until it disappeared.

Grandma always looked forward to the mailman, hoping to hear from some of her eleven children. Most of them had moved away and scattered all over the world when they were grown. My mother and Aunt Dorothy stayed around Roswell. Others would come and go. The only time Grandma had all eleven of her children together at one time was in 1960 at a family reunion in Albuquerque. They were all still alive when she died at age ninety-four.

She had "home remedies" for almost any illness or ailment. A teaspoon full of turpentine on sugar cured me from coughing at her house from then on. Sulfur and cream of tartar tablets were a must in the spring, "to cleanse the blood." I learned early on not to complain at her house. Laxatives were her specialty. They "cured" headaches, stomachaches, and cranky kids. Castor oil was the worst!

Grandma led us to believe drinking milk with fish was poisonous, and eating melons too near the rind could cause appendicitis. "Barbara Ann, that candy will give you sugar diabetes," she said, admonishing my love for sweets. Grandma had raised eleven healthy children. Who was I to question her methods; they usually worked!

I was once scolded when the iceman came to the door holding a large block of ice clasped by metal tongs, balanced on a rubber sheet spread over his shoulder. Grandma was surprised. "I don't need ice today," she said. He motioned to the large card in the front window. The top of the four colored sectioned sign said "50," meaning an order for the delivery of a fifty-pound block of ice. The other three sections were marked "100," "25," and a blank one meaning none was needed. How was a child to understand this? Once was enough after Grandma's explanation. I never bothered with it again.

It wasn't too long afterward when a new electric refrigerator was delivered. It had a funny little cooling tower on top that modern ones don't have. It was an exciting day at the Long's house. Aunt Dorothy and Aunt Arline explained to me a little man named Ya-Hootie, who could never be seen, turned the light on and off when the door was opened and closed.

Another temptation near the same front window was the tall black telephone that sat on a small table with a crocheted doily. When I picked up the earpiece, a strange voice said, "Number, please." Sometimes it asked to speak to my grandma, and later it said, "Barbara Ann, hang up the telephone." I've never quite trusted phones since then.

Aunt Arline took me downtown to the old two-story red brick telephone building across the alley from the doctor's office. We went upstairs. Wow! I saw a wooden panel with hundreds of small holes and a lady with earphones over her head saying, "Number, please," and moving little wire plugs in and out of them. There right before my eyes was the operator, my aunt's friend. She also always knew the correct time when she was asked.

When I was in grade school and needed a taxi to take me to Grandma's house, I picked up the phone in the principal's office and told the friendly operator my name and that I needed a cab. She called them for me. I just thanked taxi drivers until I learned in New York City years later they undoubtedly expected to be paid.

It was fun to go through Uncle Pat and Uncle Ray's bedroom to look at their pennant and campaign button collections on the walls. Both were Boy Scouts. The best time I had in their room was when Pat would let me blow his bugle. I knew to NEVER touch anything. Uncle Pat always tattled on me, "Mama, Barbara Ann got into my things while I was at school."

My aunts' room was much better. They were all grown up. Arline was in high school; Dorothy and Frances both had office jobs. They didn't mind if I opened their dresser drawers to look as long as I didn't touch their make-up or fingernail polish. Their fragrant room was wonderful. I especially liked the dainty perfume bottles with the rubber squeeze bulbs. My visits to the "girls' room" were soon limited to ONLY when they were at home. I vaguely remember some problem with lipstick. Well, at least I could play in the rest of the house and the yard.

Grandma wore a cotton print dress and an apron while doing her never-ending household chores. I stood on a chair and helped her at the kitchen cabinet. "Here, Barbara Ann, you grate this orange rind for me. See, just like this," as she demonstrated. She had more patience with my "cooking" than my mother did. Grandma Long made the most delicious orange chiffon cake, which she served to her Cloverleaf Club ladies. They played cards or dominoes after their meetings. She eventually went through the chairs to the top office, Noble Grand, of the Rebekahs, a branch of the Independent Order of Odd Fellows organization. I helped Grandma memorize and practice her rituals and speeches when I was a young teenager.

Her kitchen always had the sweet smell of rising yeast. Grandma often baked large loaves of fresh bread, and cut a slice for me while it was still warm enough to melt the butter she spread on it, along with homemade jam. I don't think the kitchen was very large, but the dining room next to it was. The large table always had a bowl of stewed prunes on it at mealtime. I was cautioned never to eat more than five of them nor to ever swallow the seeds or, "a tree will grow out of your ears." Once I swallowed a cherry pit just to see what would really happen. I worried less after that.

I don't recall Grandma ever being cross, but her gentle ways and frequent reminders seemed to be sufficient to keep me out of trouble most of the time. I suppose my aunts and uncles helped keep an eye on me also.

Grandma took in two or three old gentlemen boarders. They used the back bedroom with an outside entrance so they could use the outdoor bathroom. One of the old men died in his sleep one night and I was shuttled out to see the rabbits until his body could be removed early the next morning.

Grandma also took care of two "slow" children during the day. The boy, Bobby, was older than me. He spent most of his time shadowing Grandpa or talking to the trains. The girl was younger and not around as often. She just stood around. I was told to let her play with my doll and was expected to be nice to her and Bobby. Sometimes Pat pulled us in the wagon.

My aunts took me to the movies and to the New Mexico Military Institute to flirt with the cadets or to watch an exciting polo match. One of my favorite bicycle trips with my uncles was to the icehouse only a few blocks away. The man there would let us get "snow" that was left over from sawing the large blocks of ice into smaller, more manageable sizes. We made snowballs and would eat the ice in the hot summertime.

Sometimes Grandma would have us take the wagon to bring a block of ice home. She would use a sharp ice pick to break it into small pieces to use in our iced tea or lemonade glasses. Occasionally my grandmother would make a pitcher of delicious Kool-Aid. Grape was my favorite flavor.

The most wonderful treat of all was when she stirred up a batch of homemade ice cream and placed the tall metal cylinder full of the rich mixture down into an old wooden freezer and carefully placed the hand crank on top. Chips of clear ice were then dumped around inside the bucket. Coarse rock salt was slowly poured on top of the ice to make it freeze while Pat and Ray took turns cranking the handle. They let me turn it a few times, but it soon was too stiff for me to manage. It seemed ages before they called out, "It's ready. Bring your bowl and a spoon." I got to lick the dash as Grandma lifted it gently from the soft smooth tub of vanilla ice cream. Sometimes we had fresh sliced strawberries or peaches to put on top.

A skating rink was built across the street from the Longs' house. When I was old enough to cross the street alone, I walked over and watched the skaters glide gracefully across the hardwood floor on skates with large wooden rollers. Aunt Arline took me to the movies downtown in the summertime. It was only a few blocks from their house to the center of town. She and her girlfriends flirted with the usher. He gave me a box of popcorn and showed us to our seats with his flashlight. I was always careful not to touch the nasty hard dry chewing gum on the bottoms of the upturned theater seats.

A coal yard that serviced the trains and sold coal to anyone needing it was just around the corner from the skating rink. It was also a feed store. Each spring they would hatch out hundreds of baby chicks. Sometimes the owner would let me hold one. He often also had a dogie lamb or some calves to pet. It was an interesting place, but I wasn't allowed to go there alone.

When Grandma needed something from the grocery store, she would send Pat or Arline. "Take Barbara Ann," Grandma would call.

"Oh, gee whiz. Do I have to?" was usually the response. And off we would go.

Sometimes we would stop at the ice cream store on the way home for a cone. Once, when Grandma took me to the store, she let me buy a small bucket of honey. We always walked because they didn't have a car. I got to keep the pail when it was empty to gather eggs with Grandma. Uncle Ray taught me how to swing the bucket upside down over my head with water in it without it running out.

Mama took Grandma out on East Second Street to shop for fresh locally grown vegetables in the summer. The fine water mist that sprayed over the greens felt cool and nice. The aroma of freshly harvested fruits and vegetables was wonderful. We always saved the green carrot top leaves to feed the rabbits.

There had once been hundreds of acres of apple trees irrigated by large flowing artesian wells around Roswell when I was very young, but an early freeze killed most of them one spring. Cotton and alfalfa hay were the major farm crops in the Pecos Valley after the "big freeze."

The farms near Roswell were irrigated from deep Artesian wells and were green almost year-round while ranches that were located on the hills beyond the underground irrigation formation depended entirely on rain or snow. They were much drier and more barren but had a beauty all their own.

City Cousins

The Long family was larger than the Corn family, since my mother had five brothers and five sisters, but few lived near me when I was young. Most of them lived away, so I hardly knew some of my cousins on that side of the family until I was grown.

Mama's older brothers, Ross, Roy, and Charlie, all left Roswell when they finished school. They came to visit periodically, but I rarely saw them. My aunts were usually closer, except my Aunt Etta who lived and taught school in the Panama Canal Zone.

I always loved it when we got mail from Etta. It had the pungent musty smell of the tropics. She also sent photos of her family with tall stately palm trees in the background. It was really exciting when they came for a rare visit. She and Mama talked for hours and hours about living in the Capitan Mountains when they were girls.

One summer my family met Aunt Etta, Uncle Henry Leisy, and their youngest son, Ralph, in Vermont. We all shared a large country cottage near the small town of Brattleboro. They had come from the Canal Zone by boat to New York, where they bought a car. Our stay in Vermont was one of the best months of my life.

We took short trips into New York City, where I watched my first television, and Boston to see the sights. We attended several estate auctions all across the New England states. Mama was just beginning her antique decorating phase and found several treasures, including a flax spinning wheel in a dusty old box, which she bought for two dollars. I learned more about American history that summer than I ever had in school. My brother, Tom, and cousin Ralph, played together running up and down the hills covered with bright green maple trees. We all loved the "real" maple syrup and candy.

The Leisys had friends from the Canal Zone who had rented the cottage next door. They had a son, David, who was two years older than me. We got along fine. One night we went to a local western dance. I knew the dances, such as the schottische and put-your-little-foot, but they danced as fast as they talked in the East, so I really had to step it up with my Yankee dance partners.

David and I were allowed to go to the movies, but only as long as Tom and Ralph could go, too. Once he and I got to go out alone, and parked on a covered bridge after the picture show. I thought of that night again after I read the book, *The Bridges of Madison County*.

I sometimes rented a horse in Vermont and rode through the lush green countryside dressed in my white western shirt with turquoise colored buttons, and smooth-fitting Levis tucked into my fancy handmade blue top boots with my LAZY-A-BAR cattle brand on them. I also wore my large, flashy, engraved silver and gold western belt buckle. The locals knew I was NOT a Yankee.

Our trip to Vermont via Chicago on Route 66 included a detour to Niagara Falls and Canada on the way to New England. On the way back home we spent a few magnificent days sightseeing in Washington, D.C. Tom and I had to protect Mama's antique milk-glass lampshade all across the country. Dad had been right when he had told us the shells and seaweed we had collected on the beach at Cape Cod would smell bad. They soon had to be abandoned. We bought a new blue Pontiac sedan in Memphis, Tennessee. I could hardly wait to get back home and "drag Main." What a wonderful summer!

My two older Leisy cousins, Hank and Bob, were in college at New Mexico Military Institute while I was still in high school. They had never been around ranch life and were fair game for local pranks. Bob and I were riding in the pasture at the ranch when he asked me, "What kind of nuts are those?" as he pointed to the small black smooth objects lying on the ground under the bushes where the sheep stood in the shade during the heat of the day.

It was a natural reaction for me to tell him, "mountain nuts." It was all I could do to keep a straight face while he dismounted, picked one up, and put it in his mouth. I had my horse in a hard run before he was through spitting and shouting something about "getting even." He was a good sport after he cooled off.

Aunt Florence and Uncle Phil Reynolds lived in Capitan, where Florence taught school. My folks, the Dyes, and Aunt Margaret, Uncle Alton, and their children would go visit when there was a rodeo. We kids slept on the floor, which was a treat for us. We hiked up the nearby hill with a big white "C" for Capitan painted on rocks. It seemed like a mountain to us then. My cousin, Helen, was too young to go.

One summer I went to stay with Aunt Florence for a few days. She took me to a birthday party where they had delicious homemade ice cream. Someone in Capitan had typhoid fever, so she took Helen, baby Tony, and me to

Carrizozo to get shots. Later we went to a movie, but I couldn't stay awake. I rode back home to Roswell in an old limousine bus that got a flat tire, which had to be changed on the way to Grandma's house. This was a great adventure for me when I was five.

Going to the Capitan Fourth of July rodeos and visiting Aunt Florence's family was a sure thing. It often rained on us there. One year at the rodeo grounds a few miles out east of town, there was a bright red biplane giving rides for five dollars. I had that much saved up, so I went to take a ride. The pilot said I would have to bring my father. I was terribly disappointed when Dad said, "No!"

I had always enjoyed rodeos and wanted to be a calf roper. Girls could only run the barrel race, but that didn't appeal to me. I spent a lot of time at home roping and riding the milk pen calves until either the cow or Dad put a stop to it.

One of Grandma Long's "NEVER" stories came about after Tony stuck his small finger into a toy wagon tongue. When big sister, Helen, lifted the handle to pull the little red wagon, Tony screamed out in pain. The tip of her young brother's finger had been completely severed. Grandma almost outlawed wagons right then and there.

Aunt Dorothy married Thoras Dye, who came into the family with his son, Albert, who was close to my age, and his younger sister, Dotty, who lived with her aunts most of the time. They lived on a ranch not far from ours in miles, but it took half a day by car when the road was good. Sometimes we rode horses, but it still took half a day to get there. Thoras' brand was a pitchfork.

The Dyes had a large Angora goat with long twisted horns that stuck almost straight out from its head on each side. It was aptly named Handlebars. Albert and I would struggle to push and pull that stubborn critter up to the house where his dad or mine would put the two of us on its back. The goat would then run back to the barn as fast as it could go, while my cousin and I held onto its long white curly mohair coat for dear life. We did this time after time until it finally tired and refused to move. Albert and I went to school together, so I really knew him better than my other Long cousins.

Aunt Frances lived with Grandma and worked in Roswell part of the time before she married. She bought a rustic cabin at Pine Lodge in the Capitan Mountains, which we all enjoyed, especially Grandma Long. She real- ly loved the mountains. Mama took Tommy and me up to stay for a couple weeks to escape the hot summer weather at the ranch. We hiked the hills my mother knew and

loved when she was growing up. Our longest jaunt was up and over Boy Scout Mountain to a lovely waterfall where the three of us went wading after we had eaten our picnic lunch.

Another year we drove northwest over to the Smokey Bear for-est look-out tower on the north side of the Capitan Mountains, near where the well-known bear cub had been rescued from a raging forest fire a few years before. We hunted for Indian relics on a private ranch nearby. A group from the University of New Mexico was also excavating near there. Dad disapproved. He said it was like digging up someone's cemetery. Later, private excavation of Indian ruins and gravesites became illegal. The site was only a few miles from Grandma Piersol's old homestead.

Frances was a fun aunt. She had cocker spaniels and was always young at heart. She later married Uncle Bruce and raised a family of her own. Sometimes Grandma, Dorothy, Arline, Mama and I would spend the afternoon at Frances' house playing Tripoli.

Once in a while Mama and her sisters would get together and cook a delicious enchilada supper. A large plate of cheese was grated; lettuce, tomatoes, and onions were chopped while a pungent thick red chili sauce was being stewed. Corn tortillas were fried, dipped into the chili sauce, and placed on oven-warmed plates, one at a time. The final process was an assembly line, with each of the "Long girls" adding some of the prepared ingredients. This process was repeated until the "stack" of tortillas was two to four high according to each person's request. A fried egg topped the final tortilla and was garnished with tomatoes and lettuce for a very colorful and flavorful dish. Children were always served first, using a milder version of the spicy sauce.

Aunt Arline had graduated from high school and was working in 1940 when she was in the New Mexico Cuarto-Centennial program to celebrate Coronado and the coming of the Spanish conquistadors. She had to wear a long, colorful fiesta-skirt. I was so small that she was going to have me hide under the skirt so she could slip me into the program. Mama caught on and spoiled our plot. Once some of my grade school classmates and I faked an illness so we could be excused from class. We went to Arline's house, which was only a block from school to play cards until school was out. She never told on us. Perhaps she'd never even realized we had been there.

Uncle Ray was a hard worker but was a lot of fun. He got up before daylight to deliver the morning newspaper before school and tossed the Roswell *Daily Record* when he got home in the afternoon. He taught me to ride his bicycle. Ray first sat me up on the seat, but my short legs didn't even touch the pedals. He then had me stick one leg below the bars on his big bike. It was difficult and awkward leaning over lopsided, but I finally mastered riding and could hardly wait to tell my Corn cousins, Marney and Marlene.

Uncle Pat was the youngest of the eleven Long kids. He was born the year my parents married and was only six years older than I was, so sometimes we played together. Pat dropped out of school to work, then joined the Army during the Korean War. The

The Long "Girls"

first thing he did when he got home was to go back to high school to graduate. He said, "I found out I didn't know everything after all." He was a senior while I was a sophomore. We even double-dated a few times.

We had no paved walks at the ranch, so a tricycle was out of the question, but one Christmas I received a resurrected trike from the Long family to keep at their house. It was freshly painted with bright red enamel. One of the rear wheels kept coming off in spite of Grandpa's repair job, so I learned to prop the empty axle up on a tin can, get on, and pretended I was wheeling down the sidewalk at Grandma's. The next thing I knew, there I was riding just like I had dreamed. The thing was, I was leaning over to balance on two wheels. The more I practiced, the better I rode.

I carried my can so I could go to the corner, get off, turn around, then start all over, and ride back to the house. I called out to recruit an audience, but instead of the applause I had expected, Pat and his friends just laughed and made fun of me—until they all tried—but none could get the correct lean to balance the two-wheeled trike. Then, and only then, did they admire my success. I rode it that way until I started to school and the neighbor kids made fun of me. They said tricycles were for babies, but none of them were able to ride it.

One time we were all put at risk when Pat, Ray, and Arline filled a big balloon with natural gas from a jet on the back of an outside kitchen wall at Grandma's house. "Here, Pat, you hold the balloon while I fill it up. Be careful and don't you dare let go," his big brother, Ray commanded. "Arline, go get us a roll of toilet paper and don't let anyone see you. Hurry!" They then tied a long toilet paper tail to the inflated balloon. Ray held it high while Pat set the paper on fire. Ray then let it go. It floated up above the trees as the fire quickly crawled up the paper and finally, a great ball of fire. Wow! Even I knew we would be in trouble if we got caught. "Don't tell Grandma," and I didn't. We could have burned down the whole town.

Pine Lodge

Pine Lodge was a small secluded mountain resort about seventy miles west of Roswell. It was snuggled along a steep canyon on the north side of the Capitan Mountains. This is probably the only part of the Rocky Mountain chain that is faulted where it stands east and west. An attractive primitive log lodge and several cabins had been built there in 1909. Grandma Long's family had spent a few summers there many years ago, while trying to escape the heat and frequent polio epidemics of the lower valley. My mother had spent some of her teenage summers as a mother's helper there with a doctor and his young family. They all loved Pine Lodge; I did, too. I enjoyed listening to the gentle swish, swish of the breeze blowing through the pines.

Aunt Frances had a cabin but sold it when she married. The Dyes had a cabin later on. We all spent many happy hours hiking, playing in the creek and simply enjoying the rugged scenery. It was especially nice right after the regular summer afternoon thunder showers. We played cards and read at night.

There was a small natural swimming hole in the tumbling mountain stream below the lodge. It was so clear we could see rainbow trout swimming if we slipped up quietly. Mama showed me where she had stood on a rock ledge above it to dive when she was a teenager. I marveled at her bravery, since it was much too daring a feat for me to try. We kids did enjoy swimming in the cold water. The only way I could make myself get in was to simply jump right in. It felt like ice the first few seconds, but was fine once I started swimming.

When, my cousin, Marney, and I were teenagers, we sneaked a can of beer from the back porch, took it up the mountain above Frances' cabin, and drank it. We knew Mama would smell it on our breath, so we chewed some pine-sap to mask the odor. We spit and spit, but our mouths tasted like turpentine the rest of the day. My mother still scolded us about the beer.

It was the custom for the Lodge to hold dances every month or two during the summer and early fall. Most of the cabin owners, their guests, local ranchers, and folks who lived in these sparsely populated mountains would drive up the long rocky dirt road planning to stay overnight in a cabin, a tent, or in the open under the tall pine trees. There were no stores or stops along the road from town, but the pleasant aroma of pine and the cool refreshing mountain air made their half-day trip well worth the drive.

These gatherings were a major part of social life in the community, especially for those who lived in the country. Most were regulars at the dances and looked forward to seeing friends and neighbors there. These special events were not advertised, but word of mouth proved to be sufficient notice. A hat was passed around for donations to pay the band. No liquor was sold and only a few canned goods were available at the lodge, so guests brought what they wanted to eat or drink. Beer and spirits were kept in cars where most of the adults would go to "cool off" during intermissions. Loud or belligerent behavior was not tolerated.

Once a "lady" from town was flirting with one of my uncles much too much to be ignored during one of the dances, so my mother and two of my aunts gently led her out to the fishpond in front of the lodge during an intermission. They calmly told her they thought she should be baptized, "Do you prefer to be immersed or would sprinkling do?" A word to the wise was sufficient. We never saw her again.

These and other country dances were a family affair. Folks usually arrived early in the afternoon in time for a swim, waded in the small stream, or hiked the hills and enjoyed the freedom to explore. Some took the strenuous hike up to Chimney Rock, where the buildings far below looked like toys from the high vantage point. Deer were often spotted, and an occasional bear.

Black and white Gila monsters were sometimes found sunning on a rock but were avoided because of their poisonous bite. Children were told these lizards would not let go until stuck into a pail of gasoline. Rattlesnakes were scarce at this high altitude, but watching for them was a natural precaution instilled in rural people. We heard the rude warning call of blue jays and watched a timid squirrel scurry away as we hiked through the forest.

An early picnic supper was served. Fried chicken, hard-boiled eggs, pecan pie, and delicious oatmeal or molasses cookies were a welcome part of most picnic gatherings. Someone always brought jars of homemade pickles. Fresh garden tomatoes, cucumbers, radishes, onions, and green chiles were served as salad fare. Watermelon and cantaloupe were always plentiful after the first of July.

Punch and iced tea were served with whatever ice could be spared from the number two wash tubs where the beer was carefully covered by a tarp to keep it cool. Someone usually had a supply of sodas for the children as long as they promised to return the bottles, since there was a deposit refund on them. Everything tasted better in the crisp mountain air.

The temperature dropped quickly as soon as the sun set

behind the hills. Sweaters were donned and the air took on the sweet aroma of pine and piñon from the fireplaces and wood cookstoves. This meant it would not be long before the music started. Older ladies sat in squeaky rocking chairs lining the large lodge room where the dancing would soon begin. Young children ran and played on the green lawn or watched goldfish in the round pond, always under the watchful eye of a mother, grandmother, or teenage helper.

Older children walked the rock walls around the yard, slipped off to sneak a soda, or to spy on teenagers who were holding hands and trying to steal a kiss while attempting to escape numerous self-appointed chaperones. Young ladies, dressed up in attractive skirts and blouses with matching ribbons in their hair, were doing their best to act casual while flirting with the unattached bachelors, especially the handsome cowboys in their form-fitting Levis and knee-high boots that made them look even taller than they were. These young men from neighboring ranches tried to appear uninterested as they were quietly deciding which girl to ask for the first dance.

Local mountain folks usually provided music for the dance. There would be a piano, a big bass fiddle, a couple of fiddles and sometimes a guitar. The tunes were simple and varied from the waltz and foxtrot to an occasional lively hoe-down. The fiddlers started getting tuned up around eight o'clock. First the old folks and a few eager young couples started dancing across the smooth hardwood floor which had been made even smoother by a fine sprinkling of cornmeal. The fireplace had been allowed to burn down to accommodate bodies made warm by dancing. There was no need for a fire now.

Mothers danced with young sons, and fathers did a slow two-step with daughters who were just learning. Mothers introduced even the youngest to the delight of the music and the motion of dance with babes in their arms. Fathers balanced small children carefully on their sharp-toed western boots, and gracefully glided across the smooth dance floor. The tired, old and young, quietly faded away to find their beds.

Teenagers, young adults, and the middle-aged gradually livened up the dance floor with the schottische, put-your-little-foot and polkas. Now and then someone would shout, "Paul Jones," and we all changed dance partners. Everyone was acquainted by the end of the dance. The room got warmer and warmer as the crowd got more active. The group around the cars rotated in and out of the dance hall and back again to have another swig from someone's bottle of booze being passed from lip to lip without

formality, or to drink an ice cold beer from the wash-tub cooler. The echo of laughter and music filled the ever-so-dark woods until the early morning hours after the exhausted band played their final goodnight waltz.

Leftover food was placed on tables for a help-yourself bedtime snack. Soon everyone went off to bed until roused by hungry youngsters or, if lucky, awakened by the pungent smell of coffee boiling and bacon cooking over a campfire. Children cautioned to be quiet for those still sleeping paid little heed as they resumed play early the next morning.

My favorite Pine Lodge story is one Mother and Aunt Etta told about an adventure they had in 1927, when Mama was only seventeen. These two sisters had their hearts set on going to a dance at the lovely mountain lodge but had no means of getting there. So, they set out walking from their home in Roswell with very little preparation for such a long hike across miles of hot, dry rocky hills covered with mesquite, yucca, prickly pear, and cholla cacti. They took oranges to eat, water to drink, and little else.

They cut across the wide-open prairie since it would save walking several miles on the hot dusty road. They spent one frightening night at the deserted Cedar Hill Ranch, sleeping on the hard, cold, sandy ground. Aunt Etta said they heard a strange noise during the night and each reached quietly for the sharp kitchen knife they had brought along for protection. Both were so startled when their hands touched, neither of them could go back to sleep.

When it was finally light enough to see, they refilled their water jug from the windmill and slowly made their way on up through the ever more steep and rugged foothills dotted with scrub oak and piñon. They spotted a sheep-camp tent on one of the Corn ranches and were invited in for a most welcome meal, their first since they had left home. That afternoon another rancher gave them a ride part way up the rough rocky road.

They finally made their way slowly on up the difficult stair-like climb through the tall ponderosa pines, stopping every few minutes to rest their tired aching feet until they reached their destination. My mother was so tired she was ill. Both young women were totally exhausted by the time they finally arrived at the lodge.

They went to a friend's vacant cabin and helped themselves to a can of Campbell's split-pea soup and ate it cold. Etta said she had never liked it since, nor did my mother. Their feet were much too sore and swollen to get their shoes back on, much less to dance. Both just wanted to go home as they lay in bed, soon soothed to a restful sleep by the pleasant sounds of the dance music at the lodge. The two sisters caught a ride back to town the next morning. They never walked to the mountains again.

Pine Lodge and the dances held there were a happy memory in many a life from the early days for more than half a century until droughts almost dried up the stream, and television and other entertainment replaced country dances. Finally, the lodge building burned down, to end a wonderful chapter in the rural way of life.

The Corn Family

My father, Robert Irwin Corn, was a tall man with light, reddish brown hair and pale blue eyes. Dad was a natural with animals, always calm and kind. He was a quiet man, but people listened when he talked. His "No" sometimes left room for negotiation. My father was slow to anger, but when he did, his clear blue eyes looked like they could cut through steel. Dad answered my never-ending questions with short, factual replies. He rarely elaborated on any subject. The ranch was his life; much more than simply a business. Nothing on the range went unnoticed or uncared for. Someone once asked my brother what his father's hobby was. Tom replied, "That would have to be the ranch." When the same question was asked about his mother he said, "Well, I guess her hobby is my dad."

Dad was born on his parents' ranch north of Roswell at Eden Valley, not far from where his grandfather, who raised twenty-one children, mostly boys, had lived, ranched, and farmed.

My father's five brothers all had neighboring ranches when I was growing up. They provided my brother and me with a lot of cousins. There was a time when the Corn family ranches reached from the Pecos River in the east to the foothills of the Capitan Mountains in the west.

Grandpa and Grandma Corn lived in a large, white two-story frame house on a corner, only a block from Main Street. It was a quiet residential neighborhood, shaded by large cottonwood and elm trees. The side fence was covered by trumpet vines. We liked to pop the red buds before they bloomed. Dad said not to, but Grandma didn't care. She always said, "I'm going to have them pulled out," but year after year she never did.

There was a long shed along the alley, sectioned off into a chicken house complete with a few old hens, a dusty saddle house, and a three-car garage. Grandpa always had his green Chrysler coupe for the ranch, and Grandma's shiny black Chrysler sedan for town, clean and ready to go. The side road was not paved, so family all parked there in the shade of the large cottonwood trees and used the back door, even though they had to walk through the dining room and the master bedroom to get to the living room.

The living room, or parlor as Grandma called it, was long, with tall windows on the south and east sides. Several large colored prints hung from the high ceiling. A fireplace was in the center of the inside wall, but was only used on Christmas Eve. An interesting columnar black stone clock sat on the mantel, ticking as I watched, fascinated by the delicate brass gears that were visible through the glass. When I was very young, a big bear rug, head and all, stood guard over the hearth. Its big brown glass eyes and sharp ivory-colored teeth were a marvel to me.

The large room was divided by custom; one end they used and the other they didn't. Grandma sat on one side of the floor furnace and Grandpa at the other, where he could look out at the street. Grandma changed sides after Grandpa died. A telephone stand and a straight chair, as well as a large library table graced the seldom-used end of the parlor. That end of the room made it the perfect place for the Christmas tree.

A large bookcase was near the sitting area. It held photographs of all of the children, grandchildren, and later on the great-grandchildren whom Grandma was always so proud of. One drawer was dedicated to toys for the "little ones," as my grandmother referred

The Corn Family

to the younger children. I especially liked it when she would show me pictures of her high school graduating class. One girl had a black patch over one eye in which she had lost her sight when a horse had kicked her as a child. "Never walk behind a horse," my grandmother reminded us each time we looked at it.

The kitchen opened onto a large cheerful dining room with windows all across one wall. Grandma always had a white table-cloth on the table, with the sugar bowl, salt and pepper shakers, and a beautiful ruby red cut-glass holder for spoons in the center, covered with a gauze drop cloth to keep the flies off. The house was built high above ground, southern style, with a long veranda along the front and one side of the house, for coolness in the hot, dry New Mexico summers.

There were three bedrooms downstairs, and a large dormitory-style room upstairs, where Dad and his brothers had once lived while they were in high school. They had gone back to live and work on the family ranches when they left school until they married and had ranches of their own.

The kitchen was small and had limited cabinet space, but

there was a large pantry that smelled of spices. Grandchildren paused there before leaving, knowing there were cookies. Grandma always gave us some to take home.

I don't often recall seeing Grandma cook, but I do remember her ordering groceries from the store by telephone, and watching her look through the "vegetable man's" open-air produce truck as he went around the neighborhood selling fresh fruits and vegetables during warm weather. We only had canned vegetables in the winter before frozen foods were available.

The front bedroom was off the seldom-used front entry hall across from the parlor. We were never allowed to play there. It was dark, with the heavy drapes always pulled closed. It smelled musty and stale. Grandma's mother had died there two years before I was born. Years later everyone still spoke softly as though she was still there. She was always referred to as Grandma Watkins and her dead husband as Mr. Watkins, since she had remarried after Grandma's father died.

The second bedroom was a contrast to the dark mysterious one. It was light and bright. It had an outside entrance to the veranda, as well as one into the dining room. It was on the north side of the house and far away from the furnace, so it was cool or cold year round. This room always had the wonderful aroma of fruit. Grandpa used it to store boxes of local apples as well as oranges and grapefruit from the lower Rio Grande Valley. He often gave us a small bag of fruit to take home when we visited.

The master bedroom was just off the dining room at the back of the house. Grandma's dresser was neat, with a vase of long hat pins and a large hairbrush which she used to brush her waist-length gray, once blond hair, before she put it up in a bun for the day. She made it into one thick braid when she went to bed. The bathroom joined their bedroom. It had railroad style tongue-in-groove siding, a large "footed" bathtub, and the always-present gray bar of sandpaper-textured Lava soap by the lavatory.

Upstairs was the most interesting room of all. We were only allowed to go up there on rare occasions. Grandma used the stairway for storage. We kids knew it took special permission and extra good behavior to gain entry. The large upstairs room still held three double beds: two with iron frames and one with a brass frame. The small closets held trunks and shelves of treasures. Near the window stood an old sewing bust; its thin waist much smaller than Grandma's present full matronly figure. My cousins and I played make believe and dress up in the attic room.

Best of all, Marney, Marlene, and I found some of our uncles' old love letters written by high school sweethearts. We really thought they would be good for some special favors, like rides at the carnival, or a trip to the soda fountain. Were we wrong! When we approached our fathers with our blackmail attempt, Dad said in an unusually deep stern tone, "You girls didn't have any business getting into someone else's things. Just hand them to me right now. I don't ever want to hear any more about this. Do you girls understand?"

"Yes, sir," we timidly replied in unison, standing frozen in our tracks looking up at our fathers, who towered above us as we met their frigid stares. We hadn't seen this somber side of them before. We knew we had crossed the line. We never tried it again, and we never mentioned the incident to our mothers.

Reading my aunts' and uncles' old high school yearbooks was one of my favorite pastimes when I visited either of my grandparents' homes. Dad's three younger brothers, Alton, Ronald and Donald (twins), and three of his half-uncles about the same age made up a large part of the Roswell High School football and basketball teams while they were students. One year they won the state basketball championship game and rode the train to Chicago to play in a national tournament. Another year the RHS football team had completed their season without ever being scored against by an opponent. My father didn't get to participate in school sports because he had to work at the ranch.

One of my early memories as a child was of the "school-teacher" chair. It had belonged to Grandma Corn when she taught at the Eden Valley School. She had been paid $30 a month for teaching. She lived with my great-grandfather, Martin V. Corn, and his young wife whom he had married after Grandpa Corn's mother had died. Grandma had to pay $10 a month for her room and board.

My grandfather was grown, but had a lot of younger brothers and sisters living at home and going to school. This is how Grandma met Grandpa Corn and then married him in 1900.

Somehow Grandma Corn ended up with the schoolteacher's chair. She had left it behind at their Eden Valley ranch house when she moved to town, so Mama took it with her when they moved from the "Weaning House" to their Rock House Ranch. My mother painted it white. She spent the first twenty-five years of her married life painting furniture, then the next twenty-five stripping it off.

I hated that chair. It was kept on the south wall of my parents' bedroom at the ranch. I had to sit there many a time for disciplinary action when I got out of line. Mama would say, "Go sit in the WHITE chair until I say you can get down." There always seemed to be something else I would rather be doing than sitting there. The years went by and I outgrew having to sit in the chair. Mama took the white enamel off and refinished the old oak until it looked almost new. I used it at my desk.

Before my folks died, I expressed my wish to have the old chair. They both seemed to light up when they heard my request. Dad again told of Grandma coming from Texas by stagecoach to teach school. I now enjoy the antique and am glad I know its history.

The Corn family roots have been traced back to the 1400's in Holland, then Scotland and England. Their early American history began in Virginia and North Carolina before they came to Texas. Some of the family arrived in Texas while it was still a Republic. My grandfather, Robert Lafayette Corn, was only four years old when his family came to the Pecos Valley from Kerrville, Texas, in a wagon train in 1878. The trip took three long months.

Grandpa was from a large family of eight girls and thirteen boys, most of whom farmed and ranched in the area. When young, I thought all white men were uncles. They were true pioneers in New Mexico.

Grandpa Corn always wore a suit. He took his jacket off in the house, but wore his vest with his big yellow elk tooth watch fob in the pocket. He took khaki pants and shirts to their Brown Lake Ranch and changed clothes to do his ranch work. After my grandparents moved to town, Dad told me his father had gone to the barbershop every morning to be shaved.

When I was small, my grandfather held me on his lap and kissed me with his big bushy mustache that scratched my face. I hated it. He would always reach into his pocket to give me some coins. The buffalo nickels were my favorites. I rode to the Brown Lake Ranch with him one time in his green Chrysler coupe. He had apples and lemon drops. I don't remember Grandpa having much to say.

Grandpa Corn smelled like Absorbine Jr. liniment when he was old and in pain. He had gangrene in his leg caused by a foot injury, and was told he would die unless his leg was amputated. Old Doctor Lovelace flew down from Albuquerque for a consultation and confirmed what the local doctors had said. Grandpa said, "I've lived long enough," and was buried with both legs at age seventy-three.

My grandmother, Maggie Ash Corn, had roots that included some of the earliest settlers in Virginia in and around the Jamestown Colony before the Mayflower landed up north. They slowly migrated west through the Carolinas and into Texas, where Grandma was born. She graduated from high school, earned a teaching certificate, and came to New Mexico in a stagecoach to teach at the Eden Valley School in 1898.

Grandma Corn was a tall, stately woman. She wore a cotton housedress in the morning to do her cooking and cleaning before lunch, then bathed and dressed up either to "receive" or put on her wide-brimmed hat to "go calling." She said, "Ladies do not work in the afternoon." I'm sure it must have been different when she lived at the ranch and was raising six young sons.

Grandma had several unusual expressions: gathering information was "getting the particulars." When explaining someone's lack of ability, "precious little" was another of her favorites. She called the letter Z "izzard." Grandma surely knew and was proud of her Texas history.

My first encounter with danger happened when I was a toddler too young to recall it. I was a small blond blue-eyed child with an enormous amount of energy and curiosity. Grandma Corn was holding my hand walking along a fence-line where my dad and uncles were repairing a water gap that had recently washed out. The tale goes that my grandmother just barely yanked me from a huge striking rattlesnake in time to prevent a tragic and likely end to my short life. This was the first of several close calls I had with the terrifying buzz of the rattler.

Grandma learned to drive late in life. At least she drove slowly so everyone else had a fair chance of getting out of her way. Curbs meant little to her when she parked. She always maintained an extensive correspondence by mail and telephone with family and friends, including her entire high school class in Texas, until she outlived all of them at the ripe old age of ninety-eight.

I admired Grandma Corn for handling two serious physical disabilities, from which she suffered for many years. Half of her lower jawbone had to be removed after a painful overdose of radiation while she was being treated for skin cancer. This not only mis-shaped her once pretty face, but also made it difficult for her to eat and talk. Later she fell and broke a hip that failed to heal. She got up and used a walker to get around the rest of her long life. I never heard her complain. She was a very determined woman.

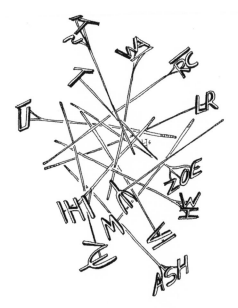

Country Cousins

There was a great deal of difficulty in getting to see and know my Long family cousins near my age, since they mostly lived far away when I was young. My Corn cousins not only all lived around Roswell, but also were from ranch families. Some were our neighbors only half a day away; others we would see at livestock sales, the fair, rodeos, and funerals.

When I was young, CORN was a common name in the Pecos Valley. I have been asked as an adult if I had been teased about the name. No one even thought of it more than once. I went to school with around twenty Corn cousins. We sometimes fought among ourselves, but outsiders beware. A grade school teacher once told me she had her class write down three common names. Smith, Jones, and Corn were on most of their papers. Our family plot at the cemetery was referred to as the "Corn Patch."

There were four Corns born the summer of 1934, all girls: Catherine, Marlene, Marilyn, and myself. Catherine, whose father, Earl, was my Dad's first cousin, lived on their family farm near Dexter, so I seldom saw her before we started to school. We then spent twelve years in the same schools.

1934 Corn Crop

Marlene was my Uncle Richard and Aunt Syble's daughter. Her brother Dick was three years older. Their BAR-RC Ranch was only six miles away but at times impossible to reach by car on the rough dirt road. When I was older, we rode horses back and forth to help work stock and to visit.

Marlene and I sometimes got to spend a few fun-packed days with each other. This was especially important for me before I started to school since I had no children my own age to play with. She and I would walk or ride our horses over miles of hills or play around Salt Creek, which ran through their ranch. It was usually dry, but once when they had a big Fourth of July picnic it rained further west and ran so high no one could cross, so we all spent the night. What fun it was for all of the children!

She and I really got in big trouble once when we decided to make a giant firecracker during the war when we couldn't buy them. It all started when the kids in town were making caps by cutting match heads off and putting them into a small nut with a bolt screwed in part way at each end. They would throw them down on the sidewalk bolt end first, and they would pop like a small firecracker. Marlene and I decided to make one too, but we used large windmill bolts that were each about a foot long and used a nut that was almost an inch diameter on the inside. We carefully added the powder we had salvaged from several shotgun shells plus a number of match heads—an extremely hazardous procedure!

When our "bomb" was completed to our satisfaction, we gently carried it up their windmill tower and dropped it on some concrete below. It made a big BANG and the bolts, which had blown apart, went whizzing by us. Our folks came running out of the house. Uncle Richard said, "What the hell was that!" It is a wonder we weren't killed. My folks loaded me up in the car before I could say goodbye and drove home in cold, dead silence, too frightened and angry to talk about it for days.

Uncle Richard and Aunt Syble lived at their ranch except during the school week when they had to be in town. She cooked and helped when there was work to do. Richard, Dick, and Marlene could always be counted on to help us, and we helped them in return. Richard also had a keen sense of humor. He was much more talkative than his brothers, and especially enjoyed cooking. He and my dad were good buddies.

Richard raised pigs, turkeys, and sometimes goats. He asked my father to help him butcher and he always shared the meat with us. Once, when they were both up in years, Dad helped Richard slaughter a fat mutton in his back yard in town. My father said they were like "two piss ants moving a brick," getting the large, heavy lamb hung up in a tree to butcher it. Dad said, "I told Richard, we're just getting too old for this."

One time Uncle Richard had spent most of the afternoon at the Green Lantern Bar and came out to go home. A local policeman asked him, "Mr. Corn, don't you think you've had too much to drink to drive home?"

Richard replied, "Son, did you ever see a drunk SOB who couldn't drive?" and the cop watched him drive off.

He and Syble cooked delicious hot spicy Mexican dishes, which they often shared with our family. Their specialties were Spanish rice with plenty of cooked onions and red chili powder, and also a mouth-watering green chile stew. It was really sad when they lost their daughter, Marlene, and her husband in a car wreck; and later when their son, Dick, and his wife were killed in an airplane crash while they were all still young adults.

My cousin, Marilyn, was born just five days after me. We always celebrated our birthdays together in August when we were children. Her brother, Graham, who was only a year older, called her Marney since he couldn't say Marilyn. Everyone called her Marn or Marney the rest of her life. Uncle Alton and Aunt Margaret lived in an old frame house on their WA-BAR Ranch on Salt Creek up the Pine Lodge Road.

They soon built a nice small rock house down by the windmill so they could tear down the old wooden house and replace it with a large rock house with a cool basement. They had a schoolroom where Margaret home-schooled Marney and Graham for a few years before they moved into town.

Their ranch was too far away for us to come and go in one day, so we always had at least one night to sleep over, which delighted me. They had a large collie named "Big Puppy" which we rode until we grew too large. We children were put to bed with Graham at the foot of the bed and our feet together. I'm sure we kicked, tickled, and giggled because one of our parents would frequently come in to tell us, "You kids be quiet and go to sleep."

I don't remember fussing or fighting, but sometimes Marn and I ganged up on poor Graham, who could hold his own against either of us separately

Marn and Babs

but didn't stand a chance with us together. Marlene and I tried to get Dick down but it took Marney also to defeat him, since he was older and larger. He mostly stayed away from us.

Graham and Marney had a gentle old gray horse named Badger that the three of us rode bareback, sometimes all at the same time. Once Marney was on him trotting back down the hill to the barn and fell off and landed on her head. Dad, Alton, and Grandpa

Corn came running up when they saw her fall. Grandpa poked her limp body with the toe of his boot and coldly proclaimed, "Well, the damn kid's dead," and walked away.

Alton picked her up and took her crying into the house, where her mother put the side of a cool table knife against the bump on her head to take the swelling away. I don't think Grandpa placed much value on girls. Thank goodness, our fathers did.

As we grew older, we saddled horses and rode for miles across their ranch playing cowboys and Indians or throwing hard green walnuts at each other. We played hide and seek from Graham, who was always a good sport. Our favorite place to play was down at the creek. We were cautioned to always watch for rattlesnakes and to listen carefully in case the creek should suddenly run down from the mountains. We were to hurry back to the house as fast as we could so we wouldn't wash away.

We played in the cool damp sand. Mama showed us how to dig a deep hole in the floor of the creek bed and watch the water slowly seep into it. "That's how the Indians found water," she told us. We had a favorite jungle area where we could act out the latest Tarzan movie or reenact Robinson Crusoe's thrilling adventures while stranded on our imaginary island. Sometimes we hunted for Indian arrowheads and pottery shards. Other times we played on the hay with Marney and Graham's frisky, small, white, dogie Angora goats and fed them milk with a bottle. They were named after the *Our Gang* movie characters. Children were expected to entertain themselves; we did.

We three once made a cave in a sand dune and played war until we tired of the game, then stomped in our fort and left for some other adventure. Our fathers came looking for us, found the sand caved in, saw rags we had left behind, and thought we were buried. They dug frantically with their hands until they were finally satisfied we were not there. When we three came strolling in, we were given a BIG lecture on the danger of making tunnels in the sand.

When we were ten or eleven, Marney, Graham, and I discovered a small cave entrance on our Rock House Ranch while we were out riding. "Look!" Graham shouted. "There's a big hole behind that

greasewood bush." Sure enough, the dark green waxy-leafed plant
some called a creosote bush left only a tiny bit of the deep hole visible as we rode by.

Wow! We
were soon all
off of our hors-
es and cau-
tiously looking
inside our
newly found
cavern, while
watching and
listening care-
fully for rat-
tlesnakes in the cool damp hole. Marn said, "It could be really big
inside. Let's look. Graham, do you have your flashlight?" He pulled
a small penlight from his pocket.

"We're going to have to hook our belts together so I can go
down," I chimed in, knowing I was the smallest and besides that, it
was on our ranch. I carefully climbed down onto a small ledge
below the bush, tightly holding onto the belts with one hand and
the dim light with the other. All I could see below me was deep,
dark space. "Give me a rock, Marn. I'll see if we can hear when it
hits the bottom." It seemed a long time before I heard it land with
a thud.

It was plain to see that we would need better equipment to do
our spelunking, so we rode back to the house to get ropes and a
flashlight. I was careful to conceal the light under my shirttail to get
out of the house undetected. Uncle Alton casually said, "You better
shut off your flashlight before you run the batteries down."

"Oh, no," I thought. Now Mama would want to know what we
were up to. We lucked out, no questions were asked.

We had visualized a magnificent cave like the Carlsbad
Caverns with gigantic stalagmites and stalactites and knew we
would be famous for our discovery of "The Corn Cave." We were
all soon making our way slowly down the rope we had tied to the
strong bush near the entrance. There was a room large enough to

WA Bar Ranch by Sidney Redfield

stand in, but nothing more than some small stalactites and a few white crickets. It was still awesome knowing we had been somewhere no human had ever been before. This was our secret adventure.

Years later when riding alone, I leaned over in my saddle to look down into the cave's entrance for snakes, when a big black turkey buzzard flew out and startled both my horse and me. It is a wonder I didn't fall off the horse into the deep hole. Sooner or later my parents learned of the cave. When I finally showed it to them Dad said, "I've been riding by here all of my life and never knew that hole was there." Tom and I were forbidden to enter it again.

We loved to climb trees. Once when Marney, Graham, and I were all up in a small oak tree, Graham yelled, "Snake," and dropped to the ground. Marn and I followed without question. We hadn't expected to find a harmless bullsnake in a tree. We had been taught to run first and fast when we saw a snake until we learned it was harmless. Aunt Margaret's baby sister had died of a rattlesnake bite; this was a serious matter for children growing up in the country.

We all grew up wearing boots, thinking the high tops might provide some protection against a deadly rattlesnake's strike. We also carried a pocketknife from age five along with instructions on how to cut an "X" over the bite so the poison could bleed out in case we, or our horses, should happen to be snake-bitten. Thank goodness, we never had to use it for that purpose, but a knife always came in handy for other things.

We swam with or without clothes every time we had the

Bar RC Ranch by Sidney Redfield

opportunity. One afternoon following a roundup at Brown Lake, all of the cousins who had helped on horseback rode down to the lake to go swimming. There were both boys and girls so I decided to swim with my clothes on. When I got home Mama scolded me for getting them wet and muddy. I explained the circumstances and ask, "Would you rather I had taken my clothes off?" Enough said.

Now and then Marney and I would go into the rock bunkhouse and help ourselves to one of the hired men's small bags of Bull Durham. We then tried to roll cigarettes. We had been told a real "pro" could roll a neat firm smoke with only one hand while riding a horse at a gallop. We girls tried our best to shake just the right amount of dry tobacco flakes from the small cloth bag and close it just like the cowboys did, by pulling the yellow string with their teeth. The last step was the only part we mastered.

Next, we would carefully lick one edge of the fragile paper to seal our "roll" in place. A small twist at each end was supposed to produce a neatly rolled cigarette. Oops, ours were always too fat or too thin. They never stayed together long enough to light and smoke. Graham finally got the hang of it and would fashion one for us. We girls weren't any more skilled at smoking than we were at "rolling our own."

One time Dad caught me smoking one of Mama's Camels I had sneaked from her pack. I was hiding in a gully not far from the house to stay out of sight and away from the wind, so my matches wouldn't blow out. I just happened to look up, and saw my father towering above me on the ditch bank scowling. "Well, Barbara, you can either have cigarettes, or cattle, but not both." I quit.

Sometimes Marney and I got to spend a few days with each other. One Saturday at our ranch, my parents and Tommy went off to check some stock at the south well. We girls knew they would be gone for a few hours, so we decided to bake a cake and surprise them. Both of us had spent most of our lives outdoors and knew little of cooking, but we decided to bake a yellow sponge cake: a real challenge for beginners.

"Hey, Babs, we don't have enough eggs." It seems it took almost a dozen.

"That's okay, I'll go to the chicken house and get some more."

We took turns cracking and trying to get most of the small pieces of shell out of the thick yellow yolks. Sugar was rationed during the war, but we knew our folks would be so pleased with our cake they wouldn't mind us using whatever it took.

I'm not sure just what we didn't do right, but our cake surely didn't puff up like my mother's always had. It was just as flat after it was baked, as it had been when we had first poured the batter into the pan. "Marn, give me a hand to get this doggoned cake out of the pan. It's stuck." After we finally pried it out, we tried to slice it for a taste. It was like a bright yellow brick. We finally managed to saw a small piece off one side. It didn't taste any better than it looked.

Reality set in; our cake was awful! Mama would NOT be happy. We decided to remove the evidence in hopes we could, "stay out of trouble," which had been my mother's last admonition as they drove off. Of course, there was the telltale grit of sugar on the floor and cabinet top. We quickly washed the dishes, fed the egg whites and shells to the chickens for recycling, and did our best to clean up the kitchen.

What to do with the petrified cake was a big decision. We took a shovel from the garage and carried the "evidence" over the hill near one of our former "playhouse" sites, where we dug a shallow grave in the hard rocky dirt and buried it. We placed a large flat rock on top to hold it down so wild animals wouldn't dig it up. We needn't have worried. A month or so later I returned, removed the stone, looked, and discovered the ants and other insects which even ate the rotting flesh off dead animals had not touched our cake.

Of course Mama asked, "What happened to all the eggs?" It was much later before she discovered the sugar shortage. I gave a full confession about fifty years later.

That evening, Marney and I went to check a trap Dad had set

to catch a skunk that had been getting into the chicken house, eating eggs, and killing a hen almost every night. One was caught and was still alive, so we started throwing rocks to kill it. The air was already strong with the acrid odor of skunk scent, but it still had more to spray at us as we began pelting it with rocks. We got closer and closer until we finally killed it.

Marn started feeling ill on the way back to the house. By the time we had reached the yard my mother smelled us coming and shouted, "Leave all except your underclothes on the yard fence to air out." She headed us straight for the bathtub and sternly instructed us, "Be sure and wash your hair," something we never did in the hard well water. By that time, Marney had to jump out of the water and throw up in the toilet. That skunk had his revenge. She went right to bed after our bath and stayed there, wasting the rest of an otherwise wonderful weekend.

Marney and Graham's house was like a second home to me. This was wonderful for me, since I was a lonely only child before I started to school. Their home was always a fun, friendly place to visit; there were always a lot of people around. Linda, Dan, and Jane were added to their family. Marlene, Marney, Graham, and Albert were some of my closest friends growing up. Marn was the closest person I had to a sister.

Margaret was an excellent cook and was always around when work was going on. It was common for them to also invite a lot of town friends out for branding and rounding up. Alton came to help us part of the time when he could get away, and Dad would go help him when he could. It was just too far to do it all of the time.

Uncle Fred's W-LAZY-H Ranch was on Salt Creek between the Pine Lodge Road and Uncle Richard's place. Fred and his two sons were at the ranch part of the time, but my cousin, Robert, was older and was always too busy with his buddies from town or with Dick for me to see much of him when we were young. Bill was around more. He sometimes rode with us on roundups since he lived close to Marlene. Uncle Fred came by or sent his hired man over to help occasionally, but he was quiet and I never knew him as well as some of the other uncles. Aunt Bea and their daughter, Rogene, were usually in town.

Uncle Donald, or Dink as he was called, looked like his twin brother Ronald, but was much heavier. He had a funny laugh and shook all over when something amused him. His brothers teased him about needing to go to the stockyard to weigh. We girls always felt sorry for his horse having to carry such a load, but he got around fast when he needed to. He would cut up with Ronald and make everyone laugh. Aunt Helen always had a baby or was going to.

Their BAR-STAPLE Ranch was next to Grandpa's Brown Lake Ranch. We rarely went to their place. Once a hired man almost burned their house down while cleaning the stove with gasoline. Mama, Tommy and I once went to help cook for the men during a coyote chase. We had to use their bunkhouse because their house had not been repaired. No one else came to help cook. We never went back.

Uncle Ronald had the Deep Well Ranch only about six miles west of us, so he frequently came to our house to help. His brand was STAPLE-R. He was always there to help us, and Dad helped him. He was friendly, joked, and told funny stories. Marlene and I usually helped him work his livestock when we weren't in school. He often said we were better help than the boys, meaning Dick and Robert, which made us feel proud.

Another time Uncle Ronald branded a heifer calf for me with my LAZY-A-BAR. I added it to my cattle herd when it was weaned. Uncle Alton and Grandpa Corn also branded calves for me for helping with their ranch work. We kids were never given cash for helping.

Ronald and Donald hired young veterans for ranch hands just after the war. They called one Lightnin' and his buddy, Thunder. Another was called Number Nine. There was never a dull moment when Uncle Ronald was around.

Moseying

My family took numerous short trips around New Mexico. They often took "short cuts" on these excursions. These diversions weren't necessarily a shorter route to our destinations, but simply ones that they enjoyed or had never traveled before. Our family was driving alone on a jaunt from the ranch to Las Vegas, New Mexico, one summer when Dad decided to drive across the prairie on a primitive ranch road somewhere north of Vaughn miles from anywhere. He assured Mama, "It'll be just fine." She was skeptical.

All was well until we came to a wide dry wash with a powdery sand bottom. Dad stopped to look. My mother advised, "Irwin, I don't think we should try it. We'll get stuck." My father could see that several sets of tracks had crossed to the other side. He didn't say a word, but started on across. We were about midway when the rear tire dug down and spun in the soft dry sand. Our car wouldn't budge an inch either forward or backward.

Dad got out to try to free the helpless Ford to the sound of my mother's "I told you so." First, he looked for rocks to place between the tire and the sand. There wasn't a single one in sight, so he gathered some branches from some small bushes nearby and put them under the jacked up wheel to provide traction. No luck. The hot summer sun beat down making the difficult task even more challenging.

Next, Dad tried to shovel the loose dry sand away in hopes of getting down to damp sand which would provide a firm base to drive out on. It was hopeless. There we sat, out in the middle of nowhere. It could be days before anyone else came down the remote road. At least Tommy and I were happily occupied playing in the sand. Our parents were beginning to discuss the possibilities of having to spend the night out near the arroyo. That thought thrilled me. Mama suddenly pointed. "Look, I think someone's coming."

It was a man riding in an old wooden Studebaker wagon pulled by a team of mules. He informed my folks that he lived a couple miles up the draw. "You all should've come to get me first. Everyone gets stuck," he reported as a matter of fact while he hitched his team to our axle. He soon had us free of the sand. Dad handed him a twenty dollar bill and we proceeded on our way down the road in chilled silence.

It takes a long time to get to a town of any size from Roswell. Albuquerque, Santa Fe, and Las Cruces in New Mexico are all around two hundred miles away, as are El Paso, Pecos, and Lubbock in Texas. It took the best part of a day to get to any of these destinations when I was a child. Mama always packed a picnic lunch to eat somewhere along the way. She usually had hardboiled eggs, fried chicken or sliced roast beef, and pecan pie which Dad called, "holding pie," since it could be served and held in a napkin.

A lone gas station out in the middle of the prairie might be the only structure for fifty miles in any direction, with perhaps the exception of a windmill. The wide-open spaces in the West seemed strange to those who lived near where there were towns or houses every few miles. We enjoyed the solitude and serenity that the distant horizon provided as we drove along, seldom seeing another vehicle.

Uncle Alton, Aunt Margaret, and the Dyes were my folks' best

friends at the ranch. They
found time to socialize. Most
summers we would plan to
take at least one camping trip
around New Mexico with
them. We frequently went to
rodeos and toured miles and
miles of interesting roads,
many still unpaved. At night
and in the winter our folks
got together to play cards and
to visit. We kids had our
games, too. Sorry, dominos,
and poker with deuces wild
were our favorites. The temptation of television had not
yet invaded our lives.

We had to wait for rain
before we could take a long
trip so there would be plenty
of water for the animals at the ranch. If it didn't rain we had to stay
home. It generally rained in July. We usually left in early August so
we could celebrate Marney's and my birthdays. We went to the
White Sands National Monument, Elephant Butte Lake, and the
Carlsbad Caverns the summer we girls were five.

Uncle Thoras put a tarp over the tall wooden sideboards on
his pickup so my three young cousins and I could all ride on top of
the big soft bedrolls. We sat with the washtub full of iced beer and
sodas, the big black cooking pots and skillets, and boxes full of groceries. We could make all the noise we wished. It was great!

Our first stop was at the Rodeo Bar just outside Capitan. Our
three vehicle caravan pulled up beside the small building standing
all alone next to a windmill out on the narrow highway. Dad said,"
"You kids stay in the pickup. We're going to get some beer to take
to the Reynolds' house. We'll be right back. You all can have a
Coke." We knew we were going to spend the night at my aunt's
home in Capitan. We also were aware we couldn't get out, because

Uncle Thoras had hooked the tailgate and sideboards so we wouldn't fall out.

We each opened a soda, discussed our dilemma, and decided we would "break out" from our makeshift "jail." Graham was the largest, so he tried to reach the latch on the outside of the gate but alas, his arms were not quite long enough. We were really getting impatient by the time we had almost finished our sodas. Sitting there waiting for our parents was a complete waste of our valuable time.

By the time our drink bottles were empty we became even more determined to escape the confines of the old Chevy truck. It became a serious challenge. We knew that all we had to do was to call out to our folks since we could see their dim silhouettes against the light in the open doorway and could hear the sound of laughter but that wasn't the point. We HAD to get ourselves out.

We all four started searching for a possible escape route. It seemed hopeless. The canvas was tied securely over the top so there was no way to slip up and under it. All of the panels were tightly bolted together. Marney finally tried to slip her head between the narrow boards. "Hey, look, you guys, I can almost get through." We all started looking for the widest opening between the smooth horizontal bars. Albert and I were smaller than the other two and soon discovered a place where we could squeeze through, and freed Marney and Graham. Just then our parents were on their way out the door and we returned to our seats with the satisfaction that we no longer felt confined.

Our parents had explored the massive cave near Carlsbad years before, when only a few people at a time could be lowered down in a large ore bucket. During our family's visit we simply walked down a trail guided by a Park Ranger, one group at a time, to view miles of spectacular formations. He lectured at scenic points of interest. The massive Rock of Ages stalagmite towered high above the awestruck gathering of tourists staring up from its base while we listened to organ music nearby playing a tune by the same name.

You could hear the "Oohs" and "Ahs" as we looked, fascinated by the ever-changing formations in the cool, damp cavern. The paper thin, translucent, curtain-like stalactites hung above our heads as we walked slowly down the path until we came to the Big Room, which was as large as four football fields. We had a fried chicken box lunch there and then continued to explore. The highlight of the trip was when we all stood quietly deep inside the cool, damp earth and were awed by the silence and total darkness as the ranger turned out all the lights. It was a truly unforgettable experience.

Most of our trips were to the beautiful cool mountains in northern New Mexico. We would pull off the road, gather firewood, and roll out our big warm bedrolls made up with wool blankets tightly rolled in a large tarp tied together with a rope; none of those wimpy looking "store-bought" bedrolls for us. My folks still had their large sheep-camp tent but did not bother taking it camping since we usually only stayed for one night before moving on down the road. Our perfect summer evening would be complete when we enjoyed a spectacular colorful western sunset. They can be incredibly beautiful.

In the late evenings we began to watch for the evening star. "I wish I may, I wish I might, have the wish I wish tonight." Mama also taught me to make a wish each time we saw a shooting star. We slept under the open sky where we could look up at the sparkling bright stars far from city lights. They looked as though you could almost reach out and touch them. Mama pointed out the Milky Way, the Big Dipper, and the North Star. We talked about God and wondered if there were others living on any of the tiny bright spots in the huge sky while we listened quietly to the coyotes yipping and howling in the distance.

Jemez Ruins

Some of our best trips were when we visited Indian villages and attended their ceremonies. Their brightly-colored costumes adorned with feathers and bells captivated me, as did the chanting rhythm of their music and dances. The Gallup Indian Ceremonial was the best of all the celebrations where Native Americans from the United States, Mexico, and Canada gathered to demonstrate their unique tribal customs. It was held in an enchanting setting of large red sandstone hills encircling their native art and beautiful silver and turquoise jewelry displays, food booths with delicious fried bread, and the large rodeo arena. This was a wonderful way for the Indians to preserve their heritage.

A colorful rodeo was held at the ceremonial each evening to test the skills of the best riders from each tribe. The Stars and Stripes along with the unique New Mexico state flag with its brilliant red Zia sun symbol against the bright yellow-gold background were both presented in the grand entry parade, followed by all of the contestants racing around the large oval arena. They were all working cowboys on or near their respective reservations.

The calf ropers gathered, ready to perform in the order they were called. The first sat anxiously on his horse behind a rope barrier that would give the young steer a head start. A flag dropped, and his sure-footed mount was in hot pursuit while the speedy contestant skillfully threw an oval lasso around the calf's neck. His well-trained cow pony immediately shifted its weight and sat back on his hindquarters and slowly backed up to keep the long lariat rope taut. The rider was off even before the horse came to a stop and was quickly headed down the tight line to flank the critter to the ground, take his short piggin' string from his tightly clenched teeth, and wrap it securely around the animal's legs so it couldn't get up. Some of the calves weighed almost as much as the riders. The cowboy with the fastest time was the winner.

Bronc riding followed, both with and without saddles. The bucking stock that had been bred and raised for rodeos and the amateur riders were each judged on how well they performed. The contestant climbed up into the chute to mount a horse whose name he had drawn from a box, pulled his black hat down almost to his ears, and signaled the judge he was ready to ride. With its head down and heels kicked up, the snorting monster headed out of the gate with only one thought in mind: get rid of the man on his back.

In order to gain points, the rider has to have his legs up ready to spur the horse on the first jump. One arm must be held high so the judge will know it didn't touch the animal. The few seconds before the buzzer sounds must seem an eternity to the contestant doing his best to stay on top of the churning equine. A "pick-up" man rides up to assist the cowboy off the still pitching bronco as soon as time is called. When the rider is thrown off before the official time is out, all that he gets is a round of applause from an appreciative audience and a sore body from landing on the hard ground.

The women's barrel race was next. Three fifty-five gallon barrels were placed in a wide triangle where highly skilled young women rode around them, one at a time, in a cloverleaf pattern. The trick is to come around each of them as closely and quickly as possible, then head for the finish line as fast as her horse can go. However, tipping a barrel over is a penalty. The girls were all seasoned horsewomen and their mounts fast and sure-footed. Those in the stands applauded their efforts.

Bulldogging a steer with a set of sharp horns takes two men: one on the far side to "haze" and keep the running animal headed in a straight path and the "dogger" who falls from his racing mount, grabs the horns, then digs his tall boot heels into the ground. He must then turn the animal's head until it falls to the ground with all four feet in the air. A flagman signals the time. Some take less than five seconds, but others break away for "no time."

The final rodeo event of the evening was bull riding. The menacing huge Brahma bulls came out of their chutes bucking and snorting. Some seemed to swivel in the middle as they unloaded most of the almost helpless riders who were tossed around like rag dolls as they tightly gripped a rope tied around the bull's belly. Only a few of the very best riders stayed on these enormous, mean animals for the full eight seconds until the judge's whistle blew.

Once a rider was on the ground, many of the giant horned bulls would turn on a dime and attack. That's where the rodeo clowns in their brightly colored shirts, baggy Wrangler jeans barely being held up with wildly decorated suspenders, and floppy old straw hats, immediately swung into action to protect the cowboy. They jumped fearlessly between the mean charging bull and the stunned and sometimes injured rider to coax it away from them. The clowns had a large wooden barrel they would hop in and out of to confuse the bull. They knew just which ones would give chase and put on an entertaining show to the delight of the spectators.

We drove across hundreds of miles of open countryside on the vast western reservations. Dad sometimes stopped to visit Navajo sheepherders or at one of the mud and stick hogans to talk about the weather and how good the grass was. I would go with him while Mama stayed in the car and read. The Indian women wore colorful long skirts, sometimes several at a time. Their massive silver and turquoise jewelry fascinated me. The black-haired girls were as interested in my blue eyes and short curly blond hair as I was with their long dark braids. They were as bashful as I was and we rarely spoke. They had a hard life indeed, but I often envied their colorful, independent lifestyle.

Northwestern New Mexico has spectacular scenery, with deep magenta mesas jutting straight up from the immense sagebrush-covered desert floor in sharp contrast to the brilliant deep blue sky above. The landscape changed every few miles as we drove along. Black volcanic lava beds snaked across the prairie. Snow-capped mountain peaks towered in the distance. I would pretend to be riding along watching for an Indian raiding party to come charging out of each narrow canyon we passed until I was jolted back to reality as we came to some of the numerous colorful billboards along Route 66. "Live! Twenty Foot Snake," "See the Petrified Cave Man," or "Ice Cold Cherry Cider." Our  favorites were the rhyming Burma Shave signs that we saw along the roads when we went into Colorado.

We saw frequent dust devils dancing across the parched land. Now and then we would see what looked like a shallow lake in front of us. Somehow it always faded away before we could get to it. Dad said it was only a mirage. The sun and sky could play strange tricks. No wonder some of the early explorers and settlers got lost and died in the desert. Mama would reflect on what a difficult time those early pioneers had had compared to our comfortable life style.

Automobiles had no air conditioning. Windows were opened

so it was not only hot, but also windy, dusty, and noisy. We didn't mind; it was all we knew. A few cars had window-mounted evaporative coolers, but they had to be frequently refilled with water, and

proved to be more bother than they were worth. It was considered a true luxury when factory-installed air conditioning became available.

Marilyn, Graham, Albert, and I were always eager to get out of the car and explore each time we stopped. As soon as the car door opened all three mothers called out, "You kids watch out for snakes." It was common for at least one of the three families to have car trouble and be stranded out on the road while our fathers tried to repair the problem or were lucky enough to find a mechanic. We always carried a chain in the trunk in case we had to be towed.

One trip something was wrong with our Ford's fuel system and we had to back up every steep hill between the ranch and Santa Fe. We camped on the hill just north of town that night to wait for the garage to open the next day. There are now homes all over that area. We kids would really tease the others whose car broke down, arguing the merits of either Fords or Chevrolets. Albert used to say, "The reason so many Fords are painted green is so they can hide in the bushes while the Chevys drive by."

Vehicles with flat tires and steaming hot radiators were a common sight along the highways. Most travelers carried an extra spare tire and either a water jug in their car or a canvas bag hanging in the front of the radiator. We always carried an empty gallon Texaco oil can in case we needed to get water from a tank or stream. A tire patch kit and a pump were necessities to repair a leak in the thin inner tubes. Some already had so many round and triangular patches they

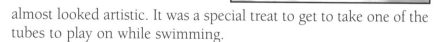

White Sands National Monument

almost looked artistic. It was a special treat to get to take one of the tubes to play on while swimming.

One summer our three-family caravan drove as far north as Colorado Springs and Denver. We toured museums, zoos, and best of all, Elitch's, a large amusement park with beautiful flower gardens where Albert, Graham, Marilyn, and I got to ride our first roller coaster. What a thrill! Tommy and Joe were so young they had to be content to ride the "bumper" cars.

One of our best camping trips was at Cowels, New Mexico, up near the head of the Pecos River. Richard, Syble, Dick, and Marlene also went on this trip, as well as our usual group. It was so cold there was frost on our bedrolls in the mornings. It was really hard to crawl out of the nice warm bed and into cold clothes, but we

soon warmed up around the fire and were ready for breakfast. Uncle Thoras made his delicious "silver dollar" hot cakes while Dad, Richard, and Alton took turns frying the bacon and eggs.

The men and children rented horses from a local wrangler and took an all-day trail ride up the steep mountain to beautiful Lake Catherine up above the timberline. There was still a little snow in patches near the mountain peak. The men all fished except Dad, who never fished. I always wanted to but never had a pole until after I was married. We girls chased the little furry marmots that stayed barely beyond our reach and watched the cute striped chipmunks playing on the rocks nearby.

It rained, snowed, and sleeted along the narrow mountain trail, so we were all wet and chilled when we got back to camp. We quickly backed up to the welcome heat of the open campfire to get warm and dry. I still think of how wonderful the fresh cool mountain air smelled and the enchanting sound of the small tumbling stream below our camp.

After the war, we began to take longer road trips. We gave up sleeping in the great outdoors for the creature comforts of motels and hotels. Aunt Margaret and Aunt Dorothy were more confined with their growing families, so Dad, Mom, Tom, and I took most of our trips without them, including trips to Yellowstone National Park and much of Colorado, Arizona, Utah, and Wyoming. We did continue to meet and have great times at each other's homes and my favorite place, Pine Lodge.

Starting to School

On the morning I turned six, I rushed to my place at our antique oak kitchen table (which was painted blue at the time) to see what my gift would be. There was a lovely blue leather pencil case with a zipper. It had my name in gold letters on the outside and held pencils that also had my name on them. Now, I was ready to go to school. There were no busses out our way when I was six, so my folks did as most ranchers did then, and moved into a house in town so Mama could send me to school during the week.

My folks first rented a small house from a little old widow who lived in a basement apartment below. I took walks with her and her big shaggy dog, Tige. This is where we lived when my brother, Tom was born.

Dad would come in on Friday and take us back to the ranch after school. I was always excited to get back home to my animals. Mama took our laundry from town so she could use the old gasoline Maytag washer on Saturday, and bring clean clothes back when we came to town Sunday afternoon.

Starting to school and having friends my age had been all I

could think of for ages. I knew my letters and a lot more from play-ing school at the ranch, but I was not prepared when my teacher, Miss Struthers, expected me to sit still at my desk most of the day instead of playing with all of the children. What a waste of my time! Sitting and paying attention was to be a lifelong struggle. I felt that every day of school was like a huge birthday party and I should be playing.

I was small for my age, so Dad had to cut a four-by-four piece of lumber for my feet to touch the floor at school. I was so small that Mama even asked the doctor if I was a midget. My mother dressed me in neatly starched, colorful cotton dresses she had made on her old second-hand treadle Singer sewing machine at the ranch. I hated having to wear dresses to school all of the time, but all of the girls did.

We had a good class. I still keep in touch with a few who are left. Catherine, Albert, Marianne, and Louise all went to Missouri Avenue School with me, or "Misery Avenue," as we liked to call our two-story red brick schoolhouse.

Marney and Marlene went to an identical building across town, Washington Avenue School. We got to go to school with each other when they stayed at my house or I stayed at theirs on occa-sion, when our mothers were needed at the ranch for special work. I don't think the teachers were very happy when we did this.

My folks bought a house only three blocks from school before summer vacation. The house was gray stucco but we had it paint-ed white. It had been built by Roswell Lumber in 1909, the year my mother was born. It had large bay windows with window seats that made a wonderful place to hide things. The kitchen sink and cabi-net top were zinc metal, and at a normal height so I could reach them (better than the high ranch cabinets). My folks had the front bedroom; the middle one was mine. As soon as Tommy got old enough, the back bedroom became his.

It was a comfortable house. My mother did some remodeling and a lot of decorating during the ten years we lived there. There was a floor furnace in the dining room. It felt wonderful to stand over it on a cold winter day. I would stand there until I could smell my leather shoe soles begin to smoke. It burned a checkered grid

pattern on the bottom of them. We had an enclosed gas heater in the in the front room and an open flame stove in the bathroom. My little brother peed on it when he was young. What a terrible odor! It lingered on and on.

We rented out the back bedroom to an Army Air Force pilot for a short time during the war. Mama turned the whole house over to two young couples one summer while we stayed at the ranch, since military people could not find housing.

Our back yard was large, with two tall honey locust trees that had fragrant white blossoms in the spring. We made a treehouse in one, with a knotted rope to climb up and down. The only problems were the sharp thorns on the smaller branches. Tommy had a sandbox full of toy cars and trucks below the treehouse. Dad made us a swing from an old tire tied to a strong limb under the other locust.

The single-car garage had two small rooms. Mama used one for storage and the other to start her baby chicks in the early spring under a warm brooder until it was warm enough for them to spend the day outside in a small pen. However, we did have to watch out for hungry neighborhood cats. The chicks were moved to the ranch when school was out. Roosters became fryers while the hens were saved to lay eggs.

Tommy made a pet of a baby chick that had been dyed green

for Easter one year. He named it Peeper. It grew into a mean white rooster and ended up on the table in a pot of Mama's delicious homemade noodles without my little brother knowing what had happened.

Mama always had a beautiful flower bed in town, since we didn't have enough water for flowers at the ranch. It was just as well, since low-growing plants would be a welcome hiding place for snakes. Mom or Dad always walked all around the yard at the ranch to check for rattlesnakes before Tommy or I went out to play when we were young.

We lived in a nice safe neighborhood in Roswell. No one needed to lock their doors except during the fair when a carnival came to town. ("Carnies" had a reputation for stealing.) There were a lot of children of all ages to play with, trees to climb, and a neighborhood store to buy milk, bread, candy, or a banana-flavored Popsicle when I had a nickel. My favorite sweets at the little store were the white candy cigarettes and the small wax bottles of colored sugar water. I could chew on the wax for hours.

Dad had our one and only car at the ranch during the week, so we walked. Few people owned cars or drove them around town as we do now. Ranch life had taught my mother how to substitute when she was cooking and didn't have all of the correct ingredients. We also always had enough food in our cabinets both in town and at the ranch to last for several weeks without having to go to the store. When we were out of bread, Mama baked. She always kept a list in the kitchen. Whoever used the last of something was to write it down for the next trip to the store. Spuds, onions, and bread were always on Dad's ranch list.

I played dolls and had tea parties with my dainty toy dishes beneath our giant lilac bush in the back yard. When Tom and I were older, we played with his toy cars and soldiers under its cool shade. I took bouquets of the fragrant violet blossoms to my schoolteachers in the spring. Mama insisted I must also take some to a teacher I didn't like. I did, but sprinkled a lot of black pepper on them, hoping to make her sneeze when she smelled them. It worked better for the Katzenjammer Kids in the comic strip than it did for me.

I had better luck with an April Fool's Day prank I pulled by putting green colored sand, which I took from a sand-painting kit at home, into a green Kool-Aid package. The fad at school was to pour a little of the sour unsweetened Kool-Aid into the palm of our hand and lick it. "Barbara, Barbara," they begged, "Can I have some, please." I generously shared with all the hands held out to me. Their smiles soon faded as they started to spit grit from their green-colored tongues. The teacher on recess duty confiscated what little was left and was about to send me to the principal's office when recess ended. I had been saved by the bell.

A fine old lady, Mrs. Bradstreet, lived next door. She was a widow, and cooked for most of the Missouri Avenue teachers at noon. I ate there once in a while when my mother was needed at the ranch to help during the week. It helped me get acquainted with my instructors, which was good since I was a very bashful child around adults.

After Mrs. Bradstreet sold her house on Missouri Avenue, she lived with my Grandmother Corn. She and Grandma always called each other Mrs. Corn and Mrs. Bradstreet, even though they had been friends for more than sixty years. They might have the "vapors," and "swoon" if they saw the lack of manners and formality today.

The Hunters lived across the street. They had a large family. Mrs. Hunter had white chickens in their back yard until the city passed an ordinance against it. They all worked around the house doing chores, but when Mr. Hunter came home from his mail route they would run out to meet him. He would play ball with all the children in the neighborhood and sometimes loaded all of us into his car to go for root beer in large frosty mugs. My, it was good.

They also had the best treehouse in the area. It had a long rope swing. We could see the top of the tall yellow brick high school building from the highest limbs of the old cottonwood tree. I loved the way Mrs. Hunter never seemed to mind so many neighborhood children coming and going through their large, white two-story house. She was always sweet to Tommy and me. One morning I went across the street before their daughter, Kim had eaten breakfast. They were out of milk, so we had red Kool-Aid on our cereal. That was terrific!

Kim was only a year younger than I was, so she came to play with me most often. We played paper dolls, jacks, and Monopoly for hours. Mama made her doll clothes. Her brother, Sammy, was Tommy's best friend. All the kids in the neighborhood would get together and play marbles, kick-the-can, hide-and-seek, spin tops, jump rope, and skate. We also played sandlot football, work-up softball, and looked for horned toads in nearby vacant lots. We shot bas-

kets at school, but goat-head stickers stuck in our ball on the dirt court. At last I had other children to play with.

Halloween was an exciting time for the children in our neighborhood. We all dressed up in colorful homemade costumes with our masks, and walked up and down the street to "trick or treat." Everyone knew us and gave us a small treat. Two nice "old maid" schoolteachers who lived across the alley from the Hunters made hot doughnuts or large molasses cookies each year. Some had us in for a bowl of popcorn. One old man gave us a trick instead of a treat; he stood on his head. His wife gave us candy anyway. Sometimes we had a citywide Halloween carnival, but we still made our neighborhood rounds until we were too old.

A woman at the end of our block came out when we knocked, but slammed the door, telling us Halloween was evil and the devil would get us. Several weeks later I rode my bicycle by her house and tossed a small paper bag of sand on her porch. It broke and made a mess. My mother was standing on our front steps when I returned home. Her hands were on her hips and she had that stern look I knew so well. "Barbara Ann, go get the broom and clean it up," she said, putting any further thoughts of throwing sand I might have had to an end.

I learned a hard, but valuable lesson walking home from school one afternoon while in the second grade. I was with several older students when we passed an empty house, and one of the larger boys started throwing rocks at an upstairs window. Soon the others were throwing too. I picked one up and threw it, far short of hitting the house or breaking a window such as the big kids were doing. Somehow I was the only one a neighbor lady recognized when she came out to chase us away. She called Miss Powell, our principal, and reported my name.

My mother met me at the door with her hands placed indignantly on her hips, not a good sign. Mama sat me down at our small kitchen table. "Were you with that bunch throwing rocks?"

"Yes," I timidly replied." "But I didn't break anything."

"That doesn't matter. You were with them. You must always get away from others when they are doing something bad or dangerous. Barbara Ann, you should have come straight home. It's wrong to take or tear up other people's property. How would you like it if someone broke our windows? Now, go to your room." I hung my head in shame. That lecture has lasted a lifetime. I don't think the others even got caught.

Years later, my brother Tom was sent back to the little store across from school to pay for a piece of candy he had picked up without paying. This lesson made an honest man of him.

One year our class was having their Easter egg hunt in the small park across from the school. I had forgotten to ask my mother to boil three eggs for me to dye to take to school. When I got to class the next day our teacher, Miss Hedrick, told us to place them in a large basket so the room mothers could hide them.

Two small hands shot up. "I forgot mine," Grant said.

"Me, too," I added. "May we go to my house to get them?"

"All right, but hurry," the teacher replied, knowing I lived nearby.

We were out the door and on our bicycles before she had a chance to change her mind. My mother wasn't home, but the house was never locked so we went right to the refrigerator to get some eggs. I knew it would take too long to hard-boil them so we decided to decorate them raw. "What can we use for paint?" my friend asked.

"I'll get Mama's fingernail polish," I replied. Soon we were making bright red designs on the cold white eggs. We hurriedly blew on them to get the sticky paint dry then made our way back to school. The teacher barely looked up as we returned to our desks.

The afternoon egg hunt went well. Everyone soon had their baskets full of beautifully decorated eggs, as well as some candy ones. One boy cracked a hardboiled egg on another's head, and the war was on. Grant and I were the only ones who knew the secret of our six red-and-white raw eggs. It didn't take long for the rest of the class to catch on as the slimy clear white and yellow goo was soon running down some of our unfortunate classmates' heads. Our teacher was upset, but didn't know who was to blame. We kept quiet and didn't get caught this time.

School was out at the end of May. We spent most of the summer at the ranch, coming to town only once or twice a month to pick up our mail and to buy groceries. We usually spent a night or two in town, visited my grandmothers, and saw a movie. One summer a neighborhood boy who lived across the alley came down with polio. Dad made the necessary trips to town alone the rest of our school vacation so Tom and I wouldn't be exposed to the dreaded disease. Cahoon Park swimming pool was closed for the rest of the season. John had to wear a metal brace on his leg when he returned to school that fall.

Grandma Long said, "That boy's lucky to be alive."

My Brother Tom

Soon after Christmas, on December 29, 1940, I had gone to bed at home while Mama and Daddy were playing cards with Aunt Dorothy and Uncle Thoras, but I awoke at Grandma's house. I had spent the night at my grandparents' many times before when my folks went to dances or took brief trips, but this was different. When I woke up, they told me I had a new baby brother and he had red hair. My father soon arrived. Part of me was caught up in the excitement but somehow I realized I was no longer the center of everyone's attention.

My mother had held me in her lap sometime shortly before I started to school and told me I was going to have a little brother or sister. I had dreamed of having a playmate as long as I could remember. Most of my cousins had siblings. I had heard stinging statements such as, "Poor Barbara, she's all alone with no one to play with," and "such a spoiled ONLY child."

The blur of activity of moving to town and starting to school filled the time. Mama had to go to see Doctor Williams and I would go with her. I liked the antiseptic smell of his office. Sometimes he would give me empty medicine bottles to play doctor with at home.

We would go to Kipling's wonderful confectionery to have a pink cherry ice cream soda or share a thick chocolate milk shake after the doctor's office visit. They had an intriguing, tall, old brass scale to weigh on, and dainty little tables and chairs. I loved going there.

Mama bought diapers and made tiny clothes for my new little brother or sister. Her friends gave her a baby shower with a lot of infant things, including a white porcelain bathtub with red trim. Mother and my aunts accumulated and arranged everything for the eagerly expected arrival. This was an exciting time. Everyone asked if I wanted a brother or a sister. I had my heart set on a girl.

The day after Tommy was born, I went to Saint Mary's Hospital with Daddy to visit. It was my mother's birthday. We took her a box of Whitman's Sampler candy, her favorite. The hospital was resplendent with holiday decorations, statues of baby Jesus, and most outstanding, the chapel with its ornate Catholic trappings. It was much more colorful than the plain Presbyterian Church where I attended Sunday School when we were in town.

A small group of nuns from the Sisters of the Sorrowful Mother in Wichita, Kansas, had come to Roswell to establish a hospital chiefly for tubercular patients, since the warm, dry air was thought to be beneficial and healing. They built a three story red brick building at the outer edge of the then small village and began treating patients of all types in 1906. The sisters still tended their own gardens, raised chickens, and had milk cows behind the hospital when I was young. Saint Mary's was where most of the local

St. Mary's Hospital

babies were born, the ill and injured cared for, and where many of the old folks died. I had been taught to be very quiet when I walked down the long wooden halls when I went with Mama to visit friends or family. Grandma told me that the tall quart juice cans full of colorful gladiolas, roses, and zinnias sitting in the hall near a patient's closed door were there because, "Some folks believe the plants will steal the oxygen and the patient will die."

All of the nurses were nuns in long black habits with only their faces and hands showing. All of the ones I remember had thick German accents and were very kind to me when I visited, as well as later on when I was a patient. For years I thought all hospital nurses were nuns. They knew my name and were anxious to show me my new little brother. I don't recall it, but my mother often said I took one look at my baby brother, Tommy, saw a red wrinkled infant, turned, and said, "Take him back."

Mama had to stay in the hospital for two weeks just because that was the custom at the time. Aunt Dorothy had a baby boy, Joe, about a week later, so Tommy had a guaranteed playmate. Later, during the war, new mothers were sent home in a week or less because of the nursing shortage. Grandma Long proclaimed, "Those women are in for trouble, getting out of bed so soon. Their insides are going to fall, just you wait and see."

I was especially disappointed that our new baby was too small and fragile to play with when he finally got to come home. I had to be careful not to touch the "soft spot" on top of his head. I could imagine my finger poking a hole through it. I did get to hold him under Mama's watchful eye and I was pleased. Now I was no longer an only child. My mother kept him in a big basket called a bassinet that she had used for me. A new blue ribbon had replaced the old faded pink one. (Tom's granddaughter used the bassinet again in 2001.)

My brother, Tom, was a quiet but mischievous child. He had our mother "snowed" when he did anything that could possibly be blamed on me. "Barbara Ann, stop that!" or "Quit picking on

Tommy," she would call out when we were away from her watchful eyes. After that I really would let him have it and fully deserved whatever punishment followed. The six years that separated us made communication and appreciation for one another difficult when we were children. Tom grew up with a keen sense of humor and was quite a tease.

In later years, when Tom was old enough to play with me, we made roads for our wagon, hiked, and played all over the ranch. We climbed on the hay in the hot dusty barn, swam, and rode horses to our heart's content. My little brother was fearless when it came to jumping from high places. He began by leaping off tall haystacks,

and progressed to being the only one either brave or foolish enough to jump off the hay shed. His other claim to fame was his ability to run barefooted across the small sharp rocks outside our fenced-in lawn. I could barely creep across without my boots or shoes.

When we were older, we were often allowed to take the pickup and Mama's old twenty-two rifle to go shoot jackrabbits late in the evening. We always found the most rabbits in our Bajillo pasture along a wide flat draw near the road to town. Tom and

Tom & Barbara – 1978

I called it the "briar patch" after Peter Rabbit's home. The dense shade of the mesquite bushes made a great place for the long-eared bunnies to shade up during the heat of the day. They hopped out to graze as soon as it cooled off. They were really numerous when we had a wet spring. Five rabbits eat as much grass as one sheep, so their population needed to be controlled. Tom was a skilled marksman.

Tom and I had been taught to drive slowly to avoid large rocks that could destroy the oil pan and ruin the engine. We also had to be careful of mesquite thorns, which caused flat tires, and of low wet or sandy places where we could easily get stuck. We did get stranded in an old washed out road-bed one time and had to walk about two miles to the house to get Dad to come pull us out.

Another evening we were twice as far from home when we got

our new red GMC pickup "high-centered" on rocks with all four wheels off the ground. We finally managed to use the jack to free it without any damage. Dad later saw our tracks across the rugged hill, and asked, "How in the heck did you kids manage to drive across there?"

Tom teased me a great deal when I was dating. "Are you going to kiss my sister? Are you going to marry her?" Tom would ask my date. He would also race to answer the phone and tell my young gentleman caller, "She's on the toilet," and hang up.

Mama sometimes told me I could go out on a date ONLY IF Tommy could go with us. My date would buy him popcorn at the movie to bribe him to sit in a different row so we could be alone. It worked. He would later tell Mama, "Barbara held hands," or "Barbara kissed." I managed in spite of his teasing.

Tom grew up learning and doing ranch work just as I had done. He soon had his SLASH-T-LAZY-S brand on an ever-growing cattle herd. Tom later bought the ranches, and still lives at the Rock House Ranch. His grandchildren are the sixth generation of Corns on a Pecos Valley ranch.

Dad and Tom

The Long Distance Club

An hour or more separated most of the ranches in this part of the country from their nearest neighbor. Visits to more distant neighbors would take half a day's drive each way on the rocky, rutted parallel track roads. A few were a full day's journey apart. Gates had to be opened and closed; rocks often had to be rolled out of the road. There was no telephone or mail service. Communications were often passed from ranch to ranch by horseback riders as work was shared.

Wives not only had their household chores to do without the benefit of electricity, but were also "ranch hands" when necessary. Many occasionally had to fill in for a sick or injured husband. Ranchers and their families took these hardships in stride. The isolation was hard on these ranch wives, who seldom got to visit with other women who understood their unique way of life.

This loneliness brought a group of seven self-reliant ranch women together in 1937 to discuss their need and desire to have more frequent contact with each other. They met and formed the Long Distance Club. Members not only helped enrich their own lives with their monthly covered-dish lunch meetings, but also

shared and supported one another through life's pleasures and tragedies. These gatherings were also attended and especially welcomed by their children, who grew up playing together, and by husbands who also had a chance to visit with one another.

Later on, when most of the women had moved to Roswell to send their children to school, meetings were held in town for the ladies only. However, the monthly family gatherings did resume in the summer. A large, mouth-watering covered-dish meal was set up and served at noon. Children got to eat first, and were back at play before the adults had finished their meal.

Afterward the men gathered to play cards or horseshoes and usually toured the host's ranch. They discussed livestock and the weather. Some of the men pitched in to help do dishes. The hostess' husband always tried to make the road more passable so people could come and go. Sometimes the whole meeting got rained out, and a few times everyone was rained in and extended the party. No one complained.

One precedent set that first year was to invite guests. Their mothers, sisters, neighbors, and friends came. The afternoon meeting always started with a prayer. Each answered roll call with a current event, a funny story, or other prearranged subjects. Ladies attended some meetings in costume, with prizes awarded to the best.

Members and children celebrating birthdays donated a penny

for each year of their age. The rest counted as the coins dropped noisily into a small metal bank. Grandmothers usually donated a dollar so no one would know just how old they were. Then, we all sang the birthday song.

The hard times of the Great Depression were reflected in the Treasurer's Report. Dues were set at only ten cents a month, "to provide appropriate small remembrances," according to the minutes. A bouquet of cut flowers cost $1; $2 bought a funeral spray when one of the charter members died during childbirth. A nightgown for an ill member was $1.25; diapers for a baby shower, $1.29; 55¢ was spent on a gift for my cousin Marlene when she was badly burned by a lighted paper jack-o-lantern. A case of Cokes was only 80¢ if the bottles were returned; 50¢

bought enough ice cream for the group, and $3.60 purchased a large Thanksgiving turkey.

The club meetings were so important to the members that Mrs. McKnight once attended while she was in early labor. Her daughter, Polly, who was born later that day, was truly a "Long Distance Club baby."

One summer it was my mother's turn to take a dessert to club. Our hens were laying a surplus of eggs, so she carefully separated the yolks and whipped the whites into a frothy foam, then slowly folded in the precious sugar saved from our small war ration allotment, along with the other ingredients to create a beautiful white angel food cake. She was pleased with the results as she took the pan gently from the oven so it wouldn't "fall," turned it over and let it cool. It was then removed from the pan and left on a plate to await the final step of applying sticky, sweet icing.

We were dressed in our best and ready to go as soon as the icing could be spread. I don't remember who let the cat into the house, but as soon as Mama stepped back through the kitchen door, she caught it in the act of taking a big bite out of the side of her otherwise perfect angel food cake. That poor critter hit the screen door so fast it didn't know what had happened. Tom and I stood watching without saying a word. Times like that, you best not even move. To say my mother was upset puts it mildly.

"Now, what will I do?" she asked herself. "Barbara, go to the chicken house and gather the eggs. I'll just have to bake another cake." The second one looked all right to me but she liked the first one better, so she cut one large slice out where the cat had been and replaced it with a wedge from the new cake. A generous layer of icing hid her skillful repair job. She swore Daddy, Tom, and me to secrecy. It was a hit; no one knew of the near disaster. Nancy, the cat (all of our cats were named Nancy) never came into the house again. At least Susie, our collie, knew she was an outside dog.

Once in a while club members would meet at a restaurant in town, and then attend a movie in the afternoon. It must have been a special treat when they all drove more than forty miles south of Roswell to Artesia to see Gone with the Wind. Husbands looked after small children at home or they were taken to a neighbors or grand-parents for the day. It was rare for a ranch wife to have a day off alone.

The ladies sewed for the Red Cross, rolled bandages, and packed gift boxes during the war. Cookies were mailed to members' sons in the service. Various money-making projects helped support a number of charities throughout the years. Caring was extended to many in the community. Boys' Ranch and the Youth Center were the main causes they helped.

At least one ranch meeting was followed by a barn dance with fiddle music provided by two of the members. One meeting in town was livened up when a fat lamb Mr. White had in his back yard in town got loose and was running around their neighbor-hood. Two of the older members of the Long Distance Club caught and penned it. The big chase even made the local newspaper. You can take the girl out of the country but you can't take the country

out of the girl.

The children always looked forward to getting together to play at the Long Distance Club meetings. The older we got, the more adventurous we became and the greater the scope of exploring the host ranch. When young, we rode lambs, then the milk cow's calf, and finally worked our way up to whichever horses we could catch. We used fences and buckets to get on, and often only had a small rope or our belts to guide the horse. One rancher was amazed when he saw Marn and me in his corral, both riding a bronc bareback that his wrangler, who had been hired to "break" horses, couldn't ride.

We explored the hills, climbed in the hay, and played "chase" to pass the time. We always returned tired and dirty, much to the dismay of our mothers who had dressed us up and always cautioned, "Don't get these clothes dirty." There was something about putting us together that seemed to encourage getting into mischief as a group which we most likely would have resisted independently, probably akin to the principles of mob behavior. My cousin Laura, who was a little older, usually stayed near her mother and once scolded Marney, Marlene, and me for being so "rowdy." We probably were, but we always had a lot of fun.

We older kids once took the younger ones to explore a cave not far from my Aunt Margaret's house. Marney, Graham and I had already been in it, but we agreed to take the younger children. We were able to walk in upright since it was all at ground level, but soon were walking stooped, as the ceiling and walls tapered into an ever-narrowing tunnel. We talked of Tom Sawyer's cave adventures as we went deeper and deeper into the bowels of the limestone hill above us.

It kept getting darker and darker as we slowly moved away from the sunlight at the entrance. I had the only flashlight, so I led the others. We were always looking and listening for rattlesnakes, which were known to frequent caves such as this. We were soon on our hands and knees, then crawling on our stomachs as the tunnel narrowed. Every now and then, I would hear a head bump, followed by "Ouch!" I could see we were about as far as we could go when my light reflected a pair of shiny eyes looking back at us.

"Stop!" I shouted. "There is something in here. Oh, my gosh! It's a skunk."

With that, everyone, including me, was trying to back up. It seemed like slow motion madness getting the youngest in the back to belly-slide backward and reverse our path through the tunnel that we were now desperate to escape. We knew the skunk could decide to run past us toward the light at any moment. Getting out into the fresh air and sunshine was a great relief. We had been fortunate the skunk had not unloaded his scent, or even worse, had been rabid and attacked us.

The Long Distance Club was less interesting to me when I was a teenager, but I was still expected to attend the family summer meetings. After lunch I got our car keys from Dad and along with the other "young ladies," as Aunt Audry kindly referred to us, drove a couple miles up the road to go skinny-dipping in Uncle Hub's dirt tank. When we arrived there, we found the boys had beaten us to it and were already in the water. They were shocked to see us, and stayed in the now muddy water since they too were without bathing suits.

We gave up our idea of a swim, but gathered up all except the boy's boots, shoes and hats, and took them to the nearest gate a half-mile from the tank, then went on our merry way. They were upset watching us take their clothes, but none were willing to expose themselves to rescue them. We later learned they made the youngest boy, my cousin Bronson, walk, clad only in his boots and hat, to retrieve their things so they could come back to the party.

The boys got even with us at our Rock House Ranch the following year.

Members came and went; some died or moved away. Around thirty ranch women were members at one time or another. All benefited from an idea conceived by loneliness. The children grew up and brought their babies to visit. Ranch roads and cars improved. There were many competing interests, so the club voted to disband in 1955 after nineteen unforgettable and fulfilling years of the Long Distance Club.

Christmas

Christmas has always been an exciting time, especially when we were children. My first scribbled letter to Santa was carefully placed in the living room wood-burning stove. Mama said the smoke would take it to Santa at the North Pole. It seemed to work, since I had gifts under the tree.

I remember only one time when we had our tree at the ranch. We carefully hung our primitive handmade decorations on the sweet smelling piñon tree my parents had cut while on a winter picnic outing with Uncle Alton's family in the mountains near Pine Lodge. It had no lights because we had no electricity. Mama and I made construction paper chains stuck together with flour and water paste. We made stars from foil she had carefully peeled from her Camel cigarette packages. They didn't sell foil in rolls then, only waxed paper.

That Christmas morning I received a tin wind-up merry-go-round and an old toy truck large enough to straddle and ride in the kitchen on the linoleum floor. It was a repainted toy of Uncle Pat's, but new to me. I loved anything with wheels. One of my favorite pastimes was building roads for toy cars and trucks in the dirt behind the house. Marbles became cattle in my twig corrals. A little imagination went a long way.

Other early Christmas gifts I recall were a stand-up blackboard that had a paper reel at the top with pictures, letters and numbers so I could play "school," and a tan wicker doll buggy with a lovely large baby doll that had blue eyes that opened and closed. I would load my buggy with my toys, including my straw stuffed monkey with the brown glass eyes which had been my bed partner since before I could remember, and have a parade inside the house circling through each room as I went.

This became my regular parade route with an imaginary crowd cheering. Best of all, there was always a peppy march tune in my head as we pranced around and around until Mama tired of the parade. Her role was to proclaim "Look! Here comes the parade." She helped pin ribbons on the baby carriage to decorate my "float."

One time I asked Mama if we could go to the fair in town. She looked puzzled since the fair was only in September. I told her the radio had said, "It would be fair today, tonight and Tuesday." How was I to know that was only the weather report?

There was always one thing certain about Christmas Eve: we and all of my father's family were expected to go to Grandpa and Grandma Corn's house for their annual get-together. Grandma always had a tree-trimming party for the grandchildren a few days before. The older kids got to help with a few of the fragile old German handmade ornaments that must have been in her family forever.

Inevitably, there was at least one string of lights that wouldn't burn until the bad bulb had been located and replaced. Robert and Dick took care of that job. Mostly we just watched and listened as she told us how things had been when she was a girl growing up in Texas. "When I was a child, our Christmas tree had candles since we had no electricity. All of our gifts were hand made," she explained. What a shame we were too young to really appreciate her colorful stories back then.

After the tree had been properly trimmed, Grandma gently took her china doll out of its timeworn box lined with faded tissue paper and carefully laid it on the draped base of the tree stand. We could look but not touch the doll except while she was holding it. I know it must have been her most prized possession. Grandma later gave her doll to Marlene, since she had been born on her birthday. After Marlene was killed, it went back to Grandma, who then gave it to my cousin Linda Ash Corn since Ash was my grandmother's middle name. (ASH was also Grandpa Corn's cattle brand and M, for Maggie, was their sheep brand.)

We all gathered at my Corn grandparents' after supper on Christmas Eve. The tree was soon loaded down with the gifts for those whose names we had drawn.

Grandma Long

Small children were cautioned not to touch. This is the only time I recall the fireplace being used. A floor furnace was the main source of heat. The floor was always cold in the high-ceilinged old house, which had been built before insulation or central heat was common. My father's family were all tall, and wore woolen clothing, so they were always warm. Of course we kids were too active to let a little chill ruin our excitement.

We were all dressed in our best. Marney and Marlene both had short dark braids looped up behind their ears and adorned with colorful plaid ribbons that matched their dresses. My silky fine short blond hair refused to hold a clip for more than a few minutes so my mother always did it up in tight pin curls. I was so tender-headed that rolling my hair was a painful ordeal. I had a new black and white taffeta dress one year which rustled when I walked and made sparks from static electricity when I took it off in my bedroom with the lights out. We three girls always looked nice as our Aunt Billie and her young son Ron had us parade by so we could appear in their home movies.

Marney, Marlene, and I always knew that we would get the

same gift from Grandma, except every doll, toy, or clothing item would be in a different color for each of us. I usually got blue, my favorite color. The same held true for our birthday gifts. I admired her fairness.

Robert, Dick, and Graham got to play Santa and pass out the gifts. One year we took one of Grandpa's large red wool shirts for Graham, stuffed a pillow in the front, and made him cotton whiskers. It was a keen idea until we decided he should go down the chimney. Thank goodness, someone heard us on the roof when a brick fell, and made us come down off the roof. I have always been afraid of heights but would go anywhere the others went just to prove I could. It is a wonder we all survived childhood.

We children were expected to perform on Christmas Eve. Each year Grandma would say, "Now gather up the little ones, it's time for them to sing." One year Robert Fred played his steel guitar. I was to recite a poem since I was taking elocution lessons, but was much too shy to present it. Afterward Uncle Richard took us up the street singing Christmas carols. Jingle Bells was my favorite since we all knew the words. Many of the neighbors invited us in for refreshments. We kids had sweets and Uncle Richard had eggnog. A few folks even gave us money. Mostly it was punch and cookies, but our uncle really had the Christmas spirit by the time we got back to Grandma's.

The adults in the Corn family were a quiet bunch. The men stood around and occasionally made a remark about the weather or needing to work on a windmill. They discussed their livestock and problems with predators such as coyotes, bobcats and eagles killing stock.

The women of the family were more talkative. Children, sewing, cooking, and books they had read were discussed, as well as current events. Ranch wives were usually eager for female companionship until they all moved into town to send their children to school, then most of them were anxious to get back to the peace and solitude of the country on weekends.

Another regular Corn get-together took place every January when my parents and all of Dad's brothers and their wives celebrated his, Aunt Margaret's, Uncle Ronald's, and Uncle Donald's birthdays with a formal dinner party. They always reserved a room at a nice local restaurant. Mama dressed up in her lovely salmon-colored gown with sparkling rhinestones and matching gloves or her green satin gown that was always my favorite. I liked the way it felt. They all went out dancing after their dinner. I spent the night at Grandma Long's.

Christmas morning was when Santa visited our house. Most of my earlier Christmases were spent with Uncle Alton and Aunt Margaret's family joining together, either at our house or theirs. We kids would come home from Grandma Corn's Christmas Eve party much too excited to settle down to sleep. We would try to stay awake so we could see Santa, but were quickly sent back to bed each time we wandered in to check the decorated tree. Marney, Graham, and I always made a pact that whoever woke up first would wake the others. "Wake up. Wake up," the first one awake would whisper to the others. "Hurry! Let's go see if Santa's come." I was usually the last one asleep and the first awake.

It was always still dark during the early morning hours when we three crept quietly into the living room to see what Santa had left under the tree. Family gifts were wrapped in colorful paper and ribbons, but Santa's gifts were left unwrapped and only had a tag with our name. This made them easy for us to spot. Graham would say, "Here, Barbara, this one's for you. Marn, here's yours." He would then discover his own. The toys left by Santa were immediately eagerly grabbed up by us and shown around the house to want-to-be sleeping parents. We were not allowed to open other gifts until everyone was up.

One year Graham and Marney got a red water spaniel puppy named Rhett Butler. Dolls, balls, wagons, and games were more common gifts. Once Graham almost caught their ranch house on fire playing with the fireplace after the wrapping paper mess was cleared away.

My very favorite Christmas was the year I was in the first grade. Mama was expecting a baby, which was something I had wished for most of my life. We had moved into town that fall so I could start to school. Mama always made special sweets for the holidays; pinwheel and icebox cookies, creamy fudge, white divinity with a red cherry or a walnut half on top of each piece, as well as her special fruit cake which all of our family and friends praised. Our tree was beautifully decorated.

My school class had cut out green construction paper trees and colored them with red, yellow, and blue balls. We had a class party with punch and cookies then sang Christmas carols. Santa came and passed out small bags of treats and gave each of us a candy cane. School recessed for a whole two weeks of winter vacation. It seemed to last forever.

There was only Mama, Dad, and me in our small rented house that year, since my mother needed to be near the hospital. My parents were still playing cards with friends the night before Christmas when they reluctantly sent me off to bed. I will never forget how thrilled I was on Christmas morning to find a beautiful oak roll-top desk and a matching swivel chair just my size, as well as a Betsy Wetsy doll dressed in clothes that matched the new school dress Mother had made for me that summer. In fact, there was a small blue trunk full of tiny print dresses for Betsy, all just like mine. Santa must have found Mama's scrap bag at the ranch.

Many pleasant hours were spent dressing and playing with the doll, which drank water from a tiny baby bottle. Then she wet her diaper and needed to be changed just like the new baby we were soon going to have. Years were spent at the desk until I outgrew it and got a real one. It became our telephone stand, then was later used by my four children, and next by all six grandchildren. My baby brother Tommy was born only four days after Christmas, so it was indeed a special time.

When we were older, Tom and I became Santa's helpers and were often in on the secrets of what gifts our parents were giving each other. Once Dad had to sneak a large easy chair into the living room for Mama, while she needed help bringing in a wheelbarrow for our father. After our own gift opening Christmas morning, we went down the street a block to Grandma Long's house, where she had moved soon after Grandpa had died.

We saw aunts, uncles, and a lot of younger cousins who were as talkative as the Corn clan was silent. Albert, the only one my age, and I usually played ball or rode our bicycles around town. The

Long family was much more boisterous and jovial than the Corns. There was often a card or domino game being played at the large dining room table. Children got to sit and watch until we learned the games, then we could join in with the grown-ups.

After our morning call at Grandma's, Dad made his famous eggnog. We children had some without the "nog." Dad always added grated nutmeg on top. He called it "fly-specks." One year Tom drank a small glass of port wine used to moisten the fruit-cakes. He threw up. Mama was upset with Dad for being so care-less.

Mama cooked and we had guests in or else we took salads and desserts to have Christmas dinner with someone else; it was usually Margaret and Alton, or the Dye family. Sometimes all three families would eat together. It was really nice to have Marney, Graham, and Albert to play with all at the same time. The adults played cards and we children played with our new gifts. We were fortunate that the weather was nearly always good enough to ride new bicycles or to play outdoors with a new ball.

Mama always canned fruit when it was in season in the summer. During the war years we had to go up the Hondo Valley to pick our own, since many of the workers had joined the military or went to work in town at the air base. I loved to go to the orchards and climb trees. Dad always helped my mother peel fruit and wash jars. My job was to help with the lids and to count as each jar lid clicked as it cooled to insure an airtight seal. The pears were my favorite. Mama always added red and green food coloring to a quart jar of each to serve along with her delicious cinnamon and clove spiced peaches made especially for our Christmas dinners.

Once, while I was in high school, it snowed enough to have a really beautiful, but rare, white Christmas just like Bing Crosby's song, *I'm Dreaming of a White Christmas*. My cousin, Bob Leisy, was in Roswell attending New Mexico Military Institute, but was out for their Christmas furlough. He especially enjoyed the snow since he had lived all his life in the tropical Canal Zone where his parents taught school. There were several large neighborhood snowball fights. We built a big snowman, as did almost everyone else in

Roswell since snow was so rare.

We always had to get back to the ranch the day after Christmas to feed and break ice on the water troughs for the animals. The fun and excitement of being with others and having all my new gifts to play with made this the one time I hated to have to return to the country. "Oh, do I have to go?" I pleaded. "Can't I stay at Grandma's?" Tommy and I were each allowed to take a toy or two with us, but not roller skates, not his new red scooter, and not my blue bicycle, since we had neither sidewalks nor paved roads.

One year Dad made a sled for Tom and me out of a twelve-inch-wide board and burned our cattle brands on it. It was really pretty. We had to wait two or three years for enough snow to get to use it. Even then, it only snowed enough to barely cover the graded road. Dad pulled our sled behind the car on our ranch road with a long rope. The road was rough and the sled turned over easily, so we did more running to catch up than actually riding it. The older we got, the shorter our Christmas vacation seemed before we had to go back to the school routine.

When I was older, there were gala parties and formal dances with romantic dates during the Christmas season, but nothing ever came near the excitement of waiting for Santa.

The Boots

There in the big front show window, all alone, were two pairs of brand new magnificent handmade boots; Dad's large black and white pair with his IHI brand and my identical small ones with my LAZY-A-BAR. How exciting! Mama and I each gave Dad a big hug.

The boot-maker sprinkled a little talcum powder in my beautiful new boots so my feet would slip right in. Perfect! We put them on. Dad put his pants over the tops. I really wanted to tuck my Levis in to show them off, but reluctantly followed my father's example. One boot had a squeak in it, but I didn't mind. I had to change back into my old boots when we got to the ranch so I wouldn't ruin my new ones. I slept with my black and white boots under my pillow that night so I could smell the leather. I knew I had to be the luckiest kid in the world.

Getting my first handmade boots had been a surprise. Dad had called, "Barbara, come go downtown with me," one morning while we were in Roswell the summer before I would start the second grade. I always liked going to the stores. My father usually went to the stately white marble First National Bank building, the Owl Drug, and Wilmot's Hardware, where they had everything from windmills to elegant crystal bowls and a fantastic toy department at Christmas time. This morning he pulled into the diagonal parking space in front of Welter's Boot and Saddle Shop on Main Street.

The old building still had a rigid wooden awning that jutted out over the sidewalk, although many stores already had the new modern crank-out canvas type of shade. There was a shoeshine stand just inside the door. It held two chairs on top of a high platform with footrests to put your boots on while a white-haired old black man applied polish with his long slender fingers. He then used a clean cotton cloth to put a fine shine on them. He would pop the rag so it sounded like a gunshot, look up at us, then flash his bright white teeth into a wide smile.

The best part of the shop was the pleasant pungent odor of leather. I always took a deep breath to inhale more of those wonderful rich aromas. Dad and I slowly worked our way past rows of saddles on wooden stands. The dark worn seasoned ones were there to be repaired. A few ornately hand-tooled new tan ones were waiting for their owners to come to town and take them home.

There were some plain, factory-built saddles for cowboys who could not afford the custom-made ones, which were a lifetime investment. A large glass showcase held rows of spurs, silver belt buckles, and sharp pocketknives. Racks of carefully hand-tooled leather belts were nearby. Some had a blank space on the back ready for the new owner's name or initials to be carved after they had been purchased.

One wall was filled with large round hatboxes and a sample of each style on display. Plain, gray Stetsons were what my father and his brothers all wore. They also had large black hats with a tall crown like those worn by the bad guys in the western movies. This was summertime, so everyone would be wearing straw hats until after Labor Day.

The most colorful merchandise items in the store were the bright hand-woven Navajo rugs that were used folded in half for a soft pad between the saddle and the horse. These saddle blankets had complex geometric designs woven in red, black, white or gray wool. They were small versions of the Indian rugs on the floor at our ranch.

There was a chair at the back of the shop for customers to sit while the boot-maker measured their feet. Dad sat down. A tall thin man came out of his work area in the back and asked my father, "Are those boots you're wearing comfortable, Mr. Corn?"

Dad replied, "Yes." So he didn't need to have a fitting. My father told him, "Make the tops white with black stitching and my brand in black. Be sure to use thick black leather for the bottoms so it won't scuff up. I want the same slanted high heels as these," he said as he held his foot up.

The main thing was to draw his cattle brand, IHI, exactly as he wanted it to appear mid-way up the top of the boot. This was the distinguishing touch that set off handmade boots, which helped separate the landowner rancher from the hired cowboy. Also, most ranchers wore their pants over their boots and ranch hands usually tucked theirs in. My father and his brothers all wore khaki pants rather than the coarse blue Levis worn by cowboys and most of the ranch children. I had learned that at an early age when someone asked, "What does your father do?" I was to reply "a rancher," never "a cowboy."

Dad stood up, satisfied with his transaction. The boot-maker would use his own special fancy stitched design that was his trademark. Ranchers could tell who had made a boot by the design, and the price range by the number of rows of thread in the artistic stitching. The more rows of stitching, the more costly the boots.

Dad took me by the hand and said, "Now, Barbara, sit down and take your boots off." I removed my old "shelf" boots, which had come from the shoe store down the street. They had plain brown tops and bottoms, and were scuffed up from running up and down the rocky hills at the ranch.

The boot-maker carefully straightened my socks and drew a perfect outline of each foot on a sheet of brown wrapping paper. He then slowly measured one foot at a time at a number of different places and quickly jotted down figures as he worked. It took a while before what was going on really dawned on me. Wow! I was going to get new handmade boots too, just like my father's.

I neatly drew my LAZY-A-BAR brand on the boot-maker's paper. No name was needed. Dad turned to the boot-maker, saying,

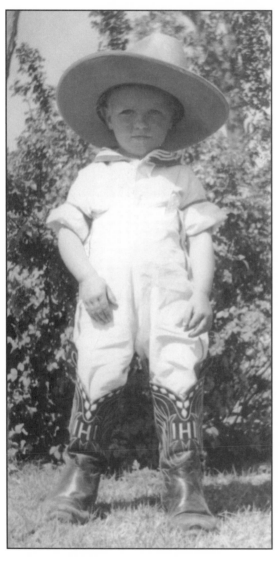

"Be sure they are ready for the fair." I could hardly wait to get home and tell Mama. She already knew but didn't spoil my excitement by saying so.

The fair meant riding in the parade, seeing the animals and exhibits, but best of all, the carnival would be there also. I loved the captivating sounds, motion, and colors of the rides; the excitement of the crowds, and the fluffy pink cotton candy. It seemed a miracle to me the way the sugar spun into tiny threads and wound its way around the cardboard cone. I liked the way the candy magically disappeared the instant it touched my tongue. Mama would take me on the ferris wheel. I loved to look at the lighted green dome of our stately old courthouse and to see how small the people below us looked when we were on the top of our exciting ride. Fair time was almost as wonderful as Christmas.

Dad had also promised I could attend the livestock show and sale with him this year: another big treat for me to look forward to.

I loved to go to stock auctions. The rancher audience sat in silence with their eyes glued to the auctioneer who had a language all his own. The only other sounds were those made by the cattle as they were led one by one into the small ring below the tiered seats that were arranged like a small opera house.

Each potential buyer had his own style of letting the auctioneer or his helpers know when they bid. It was about the only secretive act in ranching. Dad put his hands on his legs and would barely move one finger when he bid. I was cautioned early on not to move or scratch my nose. Otherwise I might buy an animal I didn't intend to. A waving hand let everyone know there was a "greenhorn" in town. Once, while still in grade school, I got to pick out a slick fat Hereford cow, bid on it, and buy it for myself at the auction. When I was older, I bought bulls.

A few weeks went by. School started, and we moved back to town with Dad coming to take us to the ranch on weekends. Mama would ask if he had checked on our boots and he replied, "They haven't even started on them."

Fair time got closer and closer—still no boots. One day my mother remarked to Dad, "Barbara's going to outgrow those boots before they are finished; they'll be too tight." I hardly slept a wink that night.

Our school's PTA was sponsoring a booth at the fair to raise money to buy playground equipment. The plan was to have local ranchers pay to have their brands burned on a large smooth pine board to be displayed in the lobby of the one and only bank in town. Dad had a long piece of lumber on our front porch and my cousin Catherine's father had another just like it at their house. They had already started soliciting and burning brands. Dad burned his, mine, and Grandpa Corn's on first.

After school the next Friday I ran all the way home as fast as my little short legs would carry me. Sure enough, our car was there so we could go to the ranch. I rushed in to change from my dress, which I had to wear unless it was so cold Mama would let me wear pants under my dress to school, with strict instructions to take them off when I got there. I'm sure she never guessed I just tucked my skirt down into them instead. I quickly put on my Levi's and ranch clothes as fast as I could. Mama had the laundry and Tommy all ready to go. The ranch seemed like home; town was just a place to live to go to school. We loaded up and were on our way.

Ordinarily we went north and bypassed downtown, but today Dad turned down Main Street and parked right in front of the boot shop. There were still a few steel rings on the curb to tie horses to in those days. That's when I first saw my beautiful new black and white boots. Now I was ready for the fair.

There was hardly ever enough moisture in arid New Mexico, but shortly before the fair it came a regular downpour. It rained and rained. At first, everyone was happy. At the ranch it meant there would be stock water and green pastures. A good thunderstorm was cause for celebration. We made delicious fudge with homemade butter that we had churned, thick cream, and pecans that Dad had picked out of the shells while listening to the radio at night. Mama also baked wonderful chewy oatmeal cookies with raisins.

As soon as it stopped raining, Dad would say, "Let's saddle up and go see how much it rained." We rode along the ridge of tall hills where we could look down upon the long, wide draws. This time it just outdid itself. The hills were saturated. Creeks started to flow and then flood. All the tanks, waterholes, and lakes were full. I had never seen so much water.

It rained off and on all that fall. Roswell's streets ran so deep with dirty brown floodwater that small boats could be seen on Main Street when the usually dry Hondo River overflowed its banks. One Friday afternoon after school we were only a few miles from our ranch house where we were planning to spend the weekend, when our Ford got stuck crossing a muddy draw.

There we were, with Dad trying every trick he knew to try to get us out of the mud, Mama holding Tommy, who was less than a year old, and me. It was getting dark and cold. Mama had brought a few bottles of milk for Tommy and had some bread and lunch-meat in the grocery bag, so we didn't go hungry.

She wrapped herself, the baby, and me up in an old blanket and some towels from the dirty laundry bag she was taking to the ranch to wash. The car had a heater, but the engine had to get hot in order for it to put out any heat, and that would have soon used what little gasoline was left. Mama was also very afraid of carbon monoxide poisoning, so we sat and slept in the cold car all night long.

Dad ate a sandwich, then set off walking to the house in the dark following the fence-line. My father had to wait for daylight after he finally arrived, then walked another few miles with a bridle and a sack of feed to find the herd of horses. He caught Mama's gentle horse, Midget, and rode it bareback while driving the others to the corral, then saddled two of them and returned to rescue us as soon as he could. Dad carried Tommy all bundled up, and I rode behind Mama hanging on to the back of her saddle as we slowly rode home. I don't recall how my father finally managed to get the car home, but he did.

On our way back to town Sunday afternoon we found the Salt Creek Bridge washed out along the highway to town, so we had to turn back. I had to miss school. Well, that surely was great news to me because I wasn't all that fond of school anyway, just of having children to play with. Mama always made me read to her out of my schoolbooks on weekends so she continued my education. I had to do my homework in my red "Big Chief" tablet by the dim light of a kerosene lantern.

I was afraid we would miss the fair. The good news was that the roads had dried up enough for us to cross the creek up west of us so we were finally able to get to town. The bad news was, it had flooded even more in Roswell and all of the long awaited events had been canceled. That meant no parade, no carnival, and no livestock auction. No place to show off my magnificent new boots. I was broken-hearted.

It seemed forever until the next fall and time for the fair.

World War II

"Extra! Extra! Read all about it. Japs bomb Pearl Harbor!" the paperboys on Main Street called out as we drove by them on our way back into town that cold December evening in 1941, after spending the weekend at the ranch. We had missed the noon news and didn't know we were at war because our radio batteries were dead. Dad bought a paper and we hurried home. I was only seven, but I knew something very bad had happened when my mother cried.

Most of the tragic impact of the event was not realized immediately. It wasn't long though before the words "RECRUIT," "DRAFT," and "DEFERRED" were added to our vocabulary. New symbols appeared; the blood-red Rising Sun of Japan and the German swastika, which was a mirror image of the one the Native Americans had woven into their rugs for many years. Our upturned arms in the daily flag salute at school looked so similar to the Germans' "Heil, Hitler" representation that we changed to placing our right hand over our heart.

Newsreels at the movies had graphic films of the European front and the war in the Pacific, including maps. LIFE magazine had stark photos of both military and civilians with sad dirty faces. These and the movies were all in black and white and at least two weeks old before we saw them. It seemed far, far away to me, but everyone was talking about the war. Lives would be changed forever.

On the way back to the ranch one night we drove northwest of town and watched night maneuvers with loud booming practice bombs, paratroopers silently gliding down, and the rapid tat-tat-tat of machine gun fire. I knew then, if we were invaded, that is how we would have to fight.

It wasn't long before we started to see and hear dozens of small blue and yellow airplanes flying over the area, training pilots who Dad said, "Didn't even look old enough to shave." Soon Roswell had an air base out at the old airport until Walker Air Force Base could be built south of town. Long rows of olive drab trucks drove up and down Main Street hauling troops. We kids waved to the solders and they waved back.

We could often see massive convoys of airplanes flying high above the ranch, in fascinating geometric patterns, sometimes too numerous to count. Uncle Pat had a set of cards with a different type of airplane or ship on each one. He soon would call out, "There's a P-40," or "Those are B-25's," every time they flew near enough to identify. We never got acquainted with the ships except what we learned at the movies.

Once, when I went to the ranch with Dad early in the morning, one of the trainers came up low behind us and buzzed, almost running our car off the road. My father was frightened and quite angry because the frisky young pilot had endangered us.

The war news was glum. We were afraid of an invasion by the German army from Mexico only two hundred miles to the south because we had heard rumors of Hitler making some sort of deal with the Mexican government to divide the United States with them after the Germans won the war. Japanese submarines had been spotted off the California coast so we were fearful they might attack from the west. Mama took my hand in hers one day and told me my father might have to go to the army. "If that happens we would have to run the ranch without him. Do you think we can do it?" she asked. I believe that must have been the moment when I grew up and knew we could do whatever had to be done. My

"V" for Victory!

mother also cautioned me, "If you see soldiers or hear shooting, ride home as fast as you can."

Fortunately my father was not drafted and we were not invaded. The war did change things though. Roswell changed from a small town where almost everyone knew each other to an ever-growing population of strangers, both military and civilian. There was an acute shortage of housing, so Roswell natives opened their homes to airmen and their families.

Patriotism was at a peak that has never since been equaled. We bought war savings stamps at school each week. They had ten-cent or twenty-five cent stamps. A book of $17.50 was good for a $25.00 bond a number of years later. (Twenty-five dollars was a lot of money in the 1940's.) The movie-theater sponsored War Bond Drives. A small submarine that had been captured was placed on display in the street in front of the Yucca Theater. A tour inside the submarine was the reward for purchasing a bond. My neighborhood friend, Warren, knew someone who worked there, so we were admitted free.

Rationing was another immediate change in our life style.

Ration books were issued to preserve war materials for the military. They also taught us to recognize the fact that there would be a shortage of goods that had previously been imported from other parts of the world. Coffee, sugar, rubber tires, gasoline, and shoes are things I recall being rationed.

Ration stamps were not needed for handmade boots, so Mama used Dad's precious coupons to buy Tommy's shoes, since he was growing fast and outgrew his little, brown, lace-up oxfords more often than stamps were issued. Some people went across the border into Mexico to buy shoes or boots to save their ration allotment, but had to leave an old pair of footwear behind and scuff up the new ones, otherwise the US border guards would still demand the prized coupons.

Cokes, candy, tobacco, chocolate, chewing gum, and new automobiles were almost impossible to buy because of the shortage. Fireworks and ammunition became scarce, as did everything made of steel or copper. Meat was in short supply throughout most of the country, but ranchers and farmers who raised their own had an advantage. Mama raised chickens, made jam, and canned fruit, so we always had plenty to eat. She traded our surplus eggs to the grocery store for credit to buy other food.

We only had one vehicle, our Ford sedan, at the beginning of the war. It almost took an act of Congress to get a new car or pickup. Used ones were repaired and kept running year after year. Dad finally bought a well-used 1941 Ford coupe from a used car lot. He took it to a shop where they removed the large trunk lid and slid an old narrow pickup bed into the back so it could be used for light hauling.

There was still a small area behind the single seat where Tom and I could sit on a padded toolbox. It wasn't great, but at least we no longer had to haul feed or sheep in our other car with the back seat removed. Believe me, people really stared when we drove down the street with a couple of horned Rambouillet rams looking back at them from the rear windows. It also freed the sedan from ranch work so Mama could now have a car in town.

The military set up bombing practice sites on a number of ranches. We had none, but there was one on a neighbor's ranch not far away. We would drive along the fence line between us to watch the twin engine airplanes dropping blue test bombs. Each held enough powder to make a small explosion so they could see where it hit, but were mostly filled with sand. The twin engine bombers flew so low we could easily see the gunner's face in the clear bubble nose cone of the airplane. We always waved at them.

Sometimes they would miss the target area with a firewall bladed around it, and catch the rancher's pasture on fire. We could see the white smoke billowing up in the distance. "Barbara, run get the tub out of the rock house," Mama would shout. We'll have to fill it with water." Dad ran to the barn to get our Indian saddle blankets and threw them into the washtub so they would soak on the way to the fire. He also gathered up shovels and a broom in case they were needed. My father made me stay home with Mama and baby Tommy when he went to fight fire. "It's too dangerous for you to go," he said. And off he went leaving a cloud of dust behind. Other ranchers did the same and fought until the blaze, which could have burned miles of precious grass, was out. Sometimes lightning started a range fire, but usually rain would put it out before it burned a large area.

Once in a while one of the low flying bombers would crash. That was a sad time. Government personnel came to haul away bodies and wreckage. They sometimes missed small pieces of metal and debris that we kids would collect and show off at school. We were interested in anything military.

Ranchers found machine gun shells, a parachute, and other "junk" the airmen lost, or tossed out of airplanes before coming back to the base. Several types of weather balloons were frequently discovered. At first ranchers returned the objects they found, but the military personnel at the base were rude and didn't seem to want to be bothered, so most gave up and kept them. They were great fun for children to play with. This continued even after the war was over.

Children stopped playing cowboys and Indians and started playing war. We dug foxholes and forts in vacant lots in town and sneaked over hills at the ranch, throwing dirt clods and rocks at the invisible enemy. Our old retired pump engine became a make-believe battle ship cruising through enemy waters destroying imaginary German U-boats or Japanese war ships. Our school's Weekly Reader kept us informed of the action overseas. We learned the names of places we had never heard of before. Anzio, Dunkerque, El Alamin, Normandy, Iwo Jima, Guadalcanal, Corregidor and many more strange places were in the news.

My small world had expanded. I felt sorry for all of the children pictured in the news and in the many war movies that were being shown. Little Margaret O'Brien's tears during the London blitz were not shed alone in the dark theater as I wiped my cheeks and saw my mother using her handkerchief too. Chiang kai-Shek's workers in China looked like endless rows of ants building countless miles of roads as they relayed thousands of baskets of stones along the human labor chain. Old bearded men, women holding babies, and young children were slowly moving along the same roads headed in the opposite direction trying to escape the Japanese bombs.

The weekly list of those killed or missing in action grew longer and longer. Our neighbors, the Hunters, had a son who was killed in the Pacific. A gold star flag was sadly placed in their front window. Dad's Uncle Wade also lost a son. We really hated the Germans and Japanese.

A large German Prisoner of War camp had been built south of Roswell near the Orchard Park farming community. We would pass by truckloads of POWs working in cotton fields as we drove into town. The farmers were short of help and most of the Germans were willing to work just to get out of camp and earn a little spending money. Years later when visiting with a friend who had been captured with Rommel's troops in North Africa and had worked as a translator on some of the area farms, Hans said, "Hitler promised us [the German army] we would march across America. He just didn't tell us we would be pulling a cotton sack."

Finally, the news came that Germany had surrendered. People celebrated, but not nearly as much as when Japan also gave up after the atomic bomb was dropped. There was no doubt about the need to drop it at the time. Everyone just wanted the horrible war to be over.

After the war, it took some time for things to change back to normal. I was seven when the war started and eleven when it ended. Everyone had either worn-out automobiles, or had none at all since the military had taken all of the industrial output during the war years. Our old 1940 Ford car, which my folks had bought new for $600 before the war, was now worth $800, after more than a hundred thousand miles of rough ranch road. We traded it in Clovis for a slightly used 1946 green Pontiac sedan with a lighted Indian-head hood ornament and stylish, white sidewall tires after we sold a truckload of feeder calves. Was I ever excited to get to drive our fancy new car!

Everything that had been in short supply gradually began to reappear. The local five and dime stores had firecrackers three for ten cents. Hershey bars, Coca-Cola, metal toys, bicycles, roller skates and marshmallows were back in the stores. Times were great. Wow! I thought I had gone to teenage heaven.

According to the news, things weren't going so well in Europe. Mama and others sent boxes of food to families in Germany of some of the nuns at St. Mary's because they were having such a hard time after the war. Sugar, bars of soap, and canned goods were included in their gift packs. They wrote thank you letters that the nuns had to translate into English. Our war was over; they were still recovering from theirs.

Chewing gum had been hard to buy, especially bubble gum. Children at school would pass gum they had already chewed to share with friends. How foolish that sounds today. One Saturday I was lucky enough to get to stay in town at Grandma Long's and go to the double feature at the Pecos Theater where they gave away Double Bubble Gum and had a bubble blowing contest up on stage between features. Albert and I went together.

We had both practiced at home. I took slow deliberate breaths through my nose and gently inflated my ever-growing pink bubble while watching others out of the corner of my eyes as one after another popped their bubble gum balloons. I came in second or third and heard the applause as I sat down, quite pleased with myself. I made the mistake of bragging about the contest at the supper table that night. "Nice girls don't go on stage," Grandma sternly proclaimed.

One of the best things to appear shortly after the war was frozen food. A frozen food locker plant was built in Roswell so we could now butcher and freeze our meat to have a year-round supply. The frozen fruits and vegetables tasted almost like they had been freshly harvested. Frozen corn, peas, and spinach were so much better than canned vegetables. Having frozen strawberries on ice cream in the winter was a special treat.

People in New Mexico were accustomed to a large number of classified military facilities, including the Los Alamos and Sandia Laboratories, and the White Sands proving ground, where the first nuclear bomb was tested. I think this fact, as well as the large number of unusual objects found on local ranches, resulted in such little attention being paid to the so-called UFO "flying saucer" when it was reported near Roswell in the late forties. My parents were not alarmed at the time, nor were our neighbors. The alleged alien crash sites have since moved and multiplied, but I still haven't seen any little green men.

The real "Space Age" history in the Roswell area occurred before the war when Dr. Robert Goddard was doing his pioneer rocket research and testing. My father had leased a pasture from Oscar White, my Aunt Syble's father, on a ranch not far from town. It was the same ranch where Dr. Goddard's rocket-launching tower and test facilities were located. Dad had watched some of the rockets being tested during the time he rented the pasture for our sheep.

Dr. Robert Goddard is considered the "father of modern rocketry." The tower and some of his equipment are on display at the Roswell Museum and Art Center.

After School

I became a Brownie Scout when I was seven: a dream come true. My friend Nannie's Aunt Kate was our leader. Our troop met after school one afternoon a week. We girls were very excited when we learned our pledge and got to wear our little brown uniforms. We sang songs and played games. As we got older, we got to "fly up" into Girl Scouts. I had always wanted to be a scout. Pat and Ray were both Boy Scouts, and Aunt Dorothy had given me her Girl Scout pin. I loved having buddies and getting to do interesting things. I was not too keen on crafts, but I loved camping.

My first overnight scouting trip was when our Missouri Avenue troop went camping for a marvelous weekend at an old, white frame house with a screened-in porch north of town near the Berrendo Draw. It stood alone on top of a small hill. There was at that time a small private lake nearby which was surrounded by cattails and other water plants. Redwing blackbirds and meadowlarks sang and chirped with delight in their lush wet environment.

The remote house had once been the gathering place for the local Ku Klux Klan. A rusty metal cross lying in the yard was the only bitter reminder of those horrific past times that we girls did

Marn, Graham & Barbara

not understand when we were young. We cooked our wieners over our campfire, then made s'mores with roasted marshmallows, which melted the Hershey bar that was sandwiched between graham crackers: a must for any Girl Scout outing. We slept on the porch in bedrolls and awoke to the sound of hundreds of cheerful birds.

Marney and I got to go to Camp Mary White in the Sacramento Mountains the summer we were ten. We were so excited! The camp was in a beautiful forest of tall ponderosa pines silhouetted against the azure blue sky. It was my first long adventure away from home and family. I went well prepared with my official Girl Scout knife and my very own flashlight.

We had a three-sided cabin that Marn and I shared with some girls from Texas, until they were frightened home by "bear" tracks which my cousin and I had made in the dust around our cabin. She and I were mostly interested in the horses. We spent our free time at the stables with the horse wranglers. They had a big Fourth of July horse show: our first. We both could outride most of the older girls and had a ball. My parents showed up unexpectedly with a load of watermelons they had bought from a farmer. It was enough to feed our whole camp. What a great day!

I went to Girl Scout camp again the next year but Marn did

not. I had ordered handmade boots that were supposed to have been finished before I was to leave town. They weren't quite ready yet, so I was extremely disappointed the morning we girls all loaded into the back of a dilapidated open truck parked down by the courthouse. We sat on our bedrolls as we set off to head toward the cool mountains through Artesia where we would pick up a few more campers.

We were almost there when some of the girls started calling to me, "Barbara, there's your mother." I rushed over to the other side of the truck. Our car was pulled alongside it, and Mama was holding a paper bag out the car window. Someone grabbed the sack and passed it to me. It was my new handmade boots, black with red tops and the LAZY-A-BAR right on the front. I was on "cloud nine."

We sang songs and chatted non-stop all the rest of the way up the final dusty graveled road, even though we had to unload once and walk so the rusty old truck could struggle up one extremely steep hill. Every night we sat around a huge campfire singing songs and telling ghost stories. Our troop had to host the final campfire, so we gathered wood and stacked it carefully to pre-pare for the last night's events. I was astonished and pleased when the counselors chose me for the honor of lighting the fire for our farewell to Camp Mary White.

One summer, Camp Mary White had a devastating forest fire and was closed for repairs. So, they held camp just outside the small picturesque mountain community of Mayhill at a former prisoner of war complex, where German soldiers either captured by the British or who had surrendered to them, had been interned before the United States declared war. My friends, Nannie, Rudell, and I went a couple days early to help sweep and set up army cots in the long barracks buildings. Mostly, we read comics until the other campers arrived.

The camp was short of water, so our leader made a deal with a local farmer for the Girl Scouts to work in his fields in exchange for him hauling water. We reluctantly loaded into his bobtail truck early in the morning to thin and weed carrots on our hands and knees. Most of the girls had never had to do any outdoor work. Nannie, Rudell, and I were almost to the end of our rows

working as the rest were barely getting started. Our goal was to escape. We quietly slipped into a chest-deep slow-moving stream at the end of the field, clothes and all, and were soon on our way back to camp. We stopped in an orchard on the way to eat our fill of little hard green apples. The farmer's son caught us but didn't mind us eating them. Our subsequent bellyaches were punishment enough.

Our drinking water was hauled in rusty fuel drums and tasted like a combination of gasoline plus the iodine that was used to purify it. No one got ill, but we surely had upset parents when we got home and told them about the water situation.

A forest ranger lived nearby. He kept a gentle milk cow in the small pasture next to our camp. "Nannie, do you think we can catch her so we can milk her?" I asked.

"Sure, but you'll have to do the milking. Rudell, come help us." Nannie was always willing to take a chance.

"Don't you think we'll get caught?" Rudell, the youngest of our group spoke up. There wasn't a reply. "Well, I'll pick some grass and leaves to feed her."

We made a long strap by connecting our belts together and tied it around the cow's neck. They fed her while I milked with one hand and held an army surplus canteen cup with the other until we each had a full cup of warm milk.

"How are we going to get it cold?" Nannie asked.

"Just drink it like it is. It's good that way," I assured her.

"Not bad," she said as Rudell and I laughed at the foamy white mustache on her face. We surely enjoyed the rich warm milk, since we hated to drink the foul-tasting water. The ranger caught on about the third evening he'd discovered that his cow had no milk and told on us.

One night we slipped out and caught one of the college-age counselors with her boyfriend. She brought us all the cherries we could eat in hopes we wouldn't tell on her. We didn't. Another time some older girls put a dead water snake in one of the cooks' beds. She was so frightened when she found it she had to be taken to the hospital in Artesia. I was blamed, but had no part of handling any snake, dead or alive.

The summer I was sixteen, Mrs. Norton took a group of Girl Scouts on a chartered plane from Juarez for a fun-filled two-week trip to Mexico. This was my first flight and I loved it. We were all extremely excited, and sang and visited all the way. The pilot let us take turns coming into the cockpit of the old DC-3 shortly before we landed and turned off all the lights so we could see the brilliant illumination of Mexico City reflected on the sparkling lake below. We were thrilled!

We did a lot of sightseeing around the city, including the famous Aztec pyramids, Chapultepec Castle, and the huge bullring where we watched a colorful Sunday afternoon bullfight. We wanted the bull to win. Our next stop was the quaint mountain village of Taxco, the silver capital of Mexico. It was, and still is one of my favorite places in the world with its narrow cobblestone streets and whitewashed houses nestled against one another under red clay-tiled roofs.

Next our chauffeur-driven cars took us on further south to Acapulco for my first look at the Pacific Ocean. The white, sandy beach was lovely, with graceful towering palms and colorful bougainvillaea growing on the tall white walls along the streets. The bright blue sky and gentle warm waves were a contrast to the rocky Atlantic coastline, and the roaring giant frigid whitecaps that I had seen in the East the previous summer. My one and only attempt at surfing came near enough to drowning me that I never again attempted it.

Our hotel was one of only four large resorts there at the time. We girls had never seen anything as ornate as the buffet tables which were decorated with ice sculptures and loaded down with fancy foods and tropical fruits. We felt like queens, having club sandwiches and drinks served on the veranda. Several US Navy ships were docked so we had more than enough male attention. What a wonderful opportunity for all of us to get to take such an exciting journey. It was a great ending for ten years of scouting.

I once had a slumber party for a few girls at our Rock House Ranch. Mom stayed in town so Tommy wouldn't bother us like she knew he would; therefore Dad became our chaperone. He couldn't understand why we teenage girls weren't ready to go to bed and turn the lights out at nine o'clock. He finally gave up on us and came to town to sleep. We played strip poker, drank Cokes, and had a great time. Dad came back to the ranch the next morning to cook an EARLY breakfast for us. He wondered why slumber did not mean sleep.

There were three high school sororities, the PALS, CHUMS, and SOS. None were affiliated with the school system. The boys had two fraternities, PARDS and FRIENDS. All five organizations had been in existence a number of years. They had "rush" and "pledge" systems modeled after those in colleges.

I joined the PALS, and made a paddle for my "big sister," La Gene. We went through an initiation where we had to eat and drink some totally disgusting concoctions guaranteed to pass through the digestive system by the time we had walked back to town after being hauled out to Six-Mile Hill. We had slumber parties, kidnap

Band Sweetheart

pajama breakfasts, teas, and dances. Best of all, we drove up and down Main Street honking, beep, beep, beeeep, beep every time we saw someone we knew.

The boys were always through with their Wednesday night meetings by the time the girls had completed theirs, and were anxiously waiting to find a date to go for a Coke, or to just hang around to meet more girls. Usually a group of boys and girls would load up into several cars and just drive around making noise. We knew we had to be off the streets by ten o'clock on a school night. Sometimes we drove through "Collins Square," the red light district. We would honk and the "ladies" would come out shouting obscenities. A few threw rocks as we spun our wheels in the gravel road. We were lucky no one got shot.

Attending high school athletic events was a major social function. Once Dad, Uncle Richard, and Uncle Alton took Marlene, Marilyn, and me to a football game in Carlsbad over a hundred miles away. We rode there and back on the "Santa Fe Centipede" as it was called. It was my first train ride. Our fathers were our favorite chaperones. They gave us money to buy tickets and food. We each had a few dollars left over. Our only instructions were to be back on the train in time to go home. Wow! We were free to run up and down the bleachers, flirt with boys, and do whatever young teenage girls do best. Later on we learned more about sports and really cheered for all of the Roswell High School teams.

The school-sponsored Girl's Athletic Association met one night a week in the gymnasium, where we were coached in basketball and volleyball by our enthusiastic PE teacher, Mrs. Whitmore. This was a most welcome diversion from our studies. Our GAA team was only allowed to take one out-of-town trip during my three years in high school. We rode the bus to a statewide volleyball and basketball tournament in Albuquerque. It was great. The boys' teams, coached by my father's Uncle Poe, went on trips all over the state to all sorts of athletic events. We girls only had one basketball to practice and play with while the boys had dozens at their end of the gym. I often "borrowed" one of theirs but had to return it when their coach appeared.

My mother told me she had once played a trombone in the Roswell High School Band. I had always wanted to be in the band, but had no encouragement at home after I had failed to practice the piano a few years before. Taking either band or chorus was mandatory in the seventh grade. My chorus teacher, Miss Seale, settled it for me when we had some kind of confrontation and I got kicked out of her music class. I could sing all right, but she demanded more time and attention than I was willing to give. My only recourse when she sent me to Mr. Villard, the principal, was to walk down the long stale-smelling hall to the band room instead.

There I met an old gentleman, Mr. Fink, who had been in World War I and had played in John Phillip Sousa's band. He was a colorful character. He smoked a big cigar in the band room, and drove his old black Model A Ford car to the Elks Club for lunch every day. He was always patient and acted like a gentleman with his students.

He was sympathetic to my cause and offered me the loan of a well-used cornet until my parents bought me a beautiful new trumpet. I was now in the band. I went to the office to let them know that I had "dropped" chorus. I met with some resistance at home but overcame it with some story about why I had been kicked out of the chorus. This was to be one of the best "bad things" that could have happened to me. I was a natural at marching, and finally able to put it to practice in real parades. The bad part was, that we almost always had to follow the horseback riders.

I made a lot of good friends. Being in the band was like belonging to a large family. The older students looked after the younger ones, and we all took up

for each other when we were frequently teased by outsiders. We rode the school bus to some of the out-of-town football games and music contests. Some of the older students would sit in the back and "neck" all the way back home in the dark. No one cared as long as we were quiet. Most of the time we were singing, *Ninety-nine Bottles of Beer on the Wall.*

One time we stayed overnight in a hotel in downtown Clovis. Some of the girls went to the boys' rooms and unrolled toilet paper from their windows down the side of the tall building. Fortunately we didn't get caught. When the boys were blamed, I told Mr. Fink, "The boys didn't do it." Nothing more was ever mentioned. We did get in trouble the time we dropped water balloons.

Finally, after years of practice, I became a first-rate trumpet and French horn player. I was in the all-state orchestra for three years. I went to band camp at Eastern New Mexico University every summer while I was in high school, where I learned to smoke terrible, strong Turkish Fatima brand cigarettes and drink Geritol health tonic, which had a high alcohol content. It was the most popular drink in "dry" Roosevelt County. Those were the worst temptations we had unless you counted kissing.

I had a music scholarship when I graduated. The band crowned me as Band Sweetheart at the Valentine Dance my senior year. I wore my beautiful deep blue strapless formal with yards and yards of satin covered with fine netting in the full long skirt. I felt elegant. Years later I played French horn in the Roswell Symphony Orchestra.

Our next door neighbors went to church on Wednesday nights, then came home and played their piano and sang long after my folks had gone to bed. Every window in their house as well as ours was wide open during the hot summer nights, since we had no air conditioner, so the music flowed freely to awaken us. We suffered in silence. My father came into my room very early one morning following their "concert" and said, "Barbara, get up and practice on your trumpet." I got out of bed, put the cold metal mouthpiece to my lips, and began to practice some warm-up scales, then played a tune or two. It wasn't long before Dad heard their windows slam shut, then came in to tell me, "That's enough." That *was* enough. We never had another late night piano recital.

Puppy Love

Many town boys hung around my house wanting to be cow-boys. Dad reluctantly took a few of them out and put them on a fencing project, one of the least glamorous jobs on a ranch. He knew a tired boy wouldn't need to be watched after dark. He was right. Most of the rhinestone cowboys washed out in one weekend. My first love fell from grace when his hat blew off and I had to get off my horse and get it for him. Dale Evans never had to do that for Roy Rogers.

I don't remember exactly how my first boyfriend evolved. It would have been Graham, but it had already been explained why cousins couldn't love cousins, well at least not as boyfriends. Boys chased girls and girls chased them back in grade school. We kissed and ran. Some liked it and some did not. I did.

Grant was my main boyfriend in the first grade. He even brought flowers to me at school. Once in the third grade the florist delivered them on Valentine's Day. The teacher put a stop to that. Most often a group of girls and boys would go to the movies with each paying their own way—"Dutch," Mama called it.

I was so small I got in free for years, then for half price until my dates were too embarrassed and paid the full price. Sometimes one boy would buy a ticket and go open the alley fire exit to let the rest sneak in. Boys bought popcorn and held their girlfriends' hands.

Going to the movies got even better after several "drive-in" theaters were built after the war. I recall the Starlite, Jinglebob, and the Ball-O-Jack: fifty cents for adults and only ten cents for children. Popcorn was a dime; a six pack of cokes in bottles was twenty cents at the grocery store so we usually took our own to the show. "Buck-a-Car Night" was the most popular evening for teenagers who needed to stretch an allowance. It was amazing how many could get into one of the old, bulky automobiles of the time. I have seen five in front and six seated in the back. There were no seat belts. It wasn't unusual for boys to ride in the trunk and then slip in with their dates in the front when tickets were full fare.

It was considered really cool to have a spotlight to shine on the theater screen before the show began to play tag with others. Every car in the park honked if the film was slow to start, or broke during the movie. It was easy to spot "lovers" in the winter because their windows would steam up.

I dated a lot of boys. The band, Rainbow Girls, and 4-H Club all had dances. Our high school had dances on Friday nights after ball games and square dancing in the gymnasium during the lunch hour. Bud, whose family had ranches north of ours, would call, "Do-se-do and around you go," as we all followed his musical instructions. The New Mexico Military Institute had hops and formal balls on Saturday nights, so there were always places to go to get acquainted with the opposite sex. Pine Lodge dances were still my favorites.

As we grew older, we each went our own way. We had lived at such a wonderful time when everyone trusted one another. We were safe on the streets and life was less complicated then than now. We just didn't realize it when we were young.

We had a bright yellow 1947 Ford pickup, which Dad had bought when he and I took a load of "old Nellie" ewes in our bobtailed truck to sell at the Fort Worth stockyard, an extremely long and hard day's drive. It was dark by the time they were unloaded. We checked into a hotel, ate, and went to a movie about the San Francisco earthquake, but I couldn't stay awake since we had left home hours before the sun came up.

The next morning we drove around Fort Worth and Dallas looking for a new pickup. After Dad had made a deal, he had to drive the bright, new, school bus yellow pickup to a loading ramp by a railroad track. I was to follow so he could load it onto our truck to haul it home. I was still only thirteen and didn't have a driver's license. I had to sit on a pillow to see to drive the truck. Dad said, "Just go slow and they'll get out of your way." They did.

When I was fourteen, I got my driver's license. Now I could finally get behind the wheel in town. I had already been using the pickup at the ranch for years. All ranch children learned to drive early so they could help feed stock, run errands, and go for help in case of an emergency. I always loved getting to take the car or pickup on errands and did so at every opportunity. My driving test consisted of old Judge Ballard asking my father, "Irwin, does she know how to drive?"

Dad said, "Yes," paid $5 for the license, and that was that.

Mama let me take the car into town to run errands. She always wondered why it took me so much longer than her. I would go by and pick up Louise, Alice, or some other girlfriend to go with me. Sometimes I would ask to go get a Coke. Dad would say, "There are Cokes in the refrigerator." That had nothing to do with me getting to drive to the Park 'N Eat or Sugar Bowl drive-ins where all the teenagers hung out.

My father certainly could not understand "dragging Main." We drove up and down the length of Main Street from Saint Mary's Hospital on the south side of town, up to NMMI on the north, honking and waving to friends along the way, a teenage ritual at the time.

Mama was much more understanding than Dad during my teenage years, or I never would have had a date. She sometimes let me stay in town with Grandma Long to attend a party or dance instead of going to the ranch for the weekend with her and Tom. Dad had to learn I would not be around home forever.

One night I got a ticket for running a red light which was still yellow when I started under it. I was so frightened, I had driven halfway home in the dark before I remembered to turn the head-lights back on. I really dreaded having to tell my parents about the ticket. They were still awake and didn't seem nearly as upset as I had expected. "You'll just have to get up in the morning and pay it."

Our yellow pickup was the only one like it in town, so my folks usually heard about it if I squealed the tires or played "ditch-em." Once I drove much too fast around the graveled circle drive at the NMMI stables, where I kept a horse and had several cadet boyfriends on the polo team. I had the pickup tipped up on only two wheels. It seemed an eternity before it finally came safely down on all fours. I was more careful after such a hair-raising close call. Thank goodness, my folks didn't hear about this reckless driving incident.

Later on we had a red GMC pickup with a horn that would stick and keep on honking. Dad showed me exactly what to do in case it happened when I was driving. I drove out East Second Street to cruise around the Sugar Bowl. I had to toot, toot, toot two or three times for "curb-service" to get it to stick, then got out confi-dently to prove how a ranch girl could handle the situation. Oops, I hadn't learned how to raise the hood to get to the horn. My cousin, Edwin, came to my red-faced rescue. He was always tops in my book from then on. It never paid to show off.

My parents had attended the New Mexico Wool Growers' Convention for several years. Tommy and I always stayed at Grandma Long's house, since the meeting was in February and we had to go to school. This was about the only important event I had been excluded from, but it was for adults only. "You're not old enough yet." Finally, while in my first year in high school, I was told I could go to Albuquerque to this long-awaited event. I was so excited I could hardly wait.

Alas, sometime in January I got ill. I had the mumps, first on one side of my face, and then on the other. I felt rotten from my ill-ness, but even worse, my heart was broken from missing my long anticipated trip. Mama took me to Aunt Frances' house to conva-lesce, since I was a little too swollen to start back to school, but did-n't feel like staying in bed. I had already become well acquainted with the afternoon radio programs such as *The Lone Ranger*, *Fibber Magee and Molly*, and *The Shadow* while confined to bed.

Bless her heart, Aunt Frances put her old manual typewriter on a card-table, along with her high school typing book, and gave me the only typing lessons I've had to date. It helped pass the time and made me feel less sorry for myself. I was already looking forward to going to the convention the following year.

I had a busy schedule my junior year in high school, but I was really excited about going to the Wool Growers' Convention in February. Susie, whose family were also ranchers, and I were the only teenage girls from Roswell to attend the convention, so we roomed together. A number of high school and college boys from Roswell High and NMMI were there. She and I were the uncontested belles of the ball. We had at least a dozen young men at our beck and call.

One afternoon, one of our polo-player buddies from the "Hill," as the Military Institute was called, came to our room at the Hilton. He was smoking a big black cigar. When we heard our folks knocking on the door, we were afraid they would be upset if they found a "man" in our room, so we hurriedly sent the worried cadet to stand in the bathtub with the shower curtain pulled. Dad went into the bathroom almost as soon as they got inside our room, washed his hands, and came out without saying a word. My father turned as they were finally leaving and said, "I think you better let that boy out of the bathroom. He's about to choke on his cigar."

I had enough fun to make up for missing the Wool Growers' Convention the year before. My picture appeared in The Albuquerque *Journal* in my ever-so-stylish white wool suit attending the ladies' tea and style show. This was my first major introduction to formal adult socializing.

My folks had attended the gala New Year's Eve party at the Chinese Palace in Juarez, Mexico with Aunt Margaret and Uncle Alton during my junior year in high school. They went to ride in the El Paso, Texas Sun Bowl Parade on New Year's Day with the Chaves County Sheriff's Posse, just across the Rio Grande River from Juarez. They had such a good time they wanted to go again the following year.

By the time school started in the fall of my senior year, Marney was engaged to Jerry, Graham to Connie, and I was betrothed to Harold. I suppose our folks figured the only way for them to go back to El Paso for the New Year's festivities again, and to also see that we three young couples were all properly chaperoned, was to take us along. New Year's Eve in Juarez sounded like a great idea!

My parents made all of the reservations, including tickets to the New Year's Day Sun Bowl football game. The three boys shared a room at one end of the motel while we girls bunked in a room near our parents. Margaret's sister, Martha, and her husband also stayed near us.

We had an elegant steak and lobster dinner at the Chinese Palace before the show began. The club was decorated with balloons and streamers. The red and gold silk decor was certainly more elaborate than in any of our Roswell restaurants. We were not disappointed with the fast-moving floorshow at the Palace, which featured several singers, Mexican folk dancers, a magician, a large troop of Chinese contortionists, and a western singer.

The emcee was full of jokes that got more off-color as the evening went on. The contortionists twisted themselves into shapes I am convinced the human body is not intended to assume. They stacked chairs, dishes, and each other almost to the ceiling while the fully-packed room applauded. The western singer came out and sang *Mule Train*, *Shrimp Boats Are Coming*, and our favorite, *Slow*

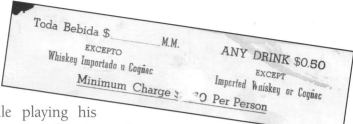

Poke, while playing his
guitar. He was our favorite performer.

Hats, horns, champagne, and confetti were distributed. Everyone was feeling cheerful as the balloons fell from the ceiling of the dance hall at midnight. We all shouted, "Happy New Year!" as the band played *Auld Lang Syne*. We kissed and kissed, then kissed some more.

The show resumed after a short intermission. We then heard more of *Slow Poke*, but the singer's voice kept getting more hoarse as he sipped his drink in the now smoke-filled room. The music finally played out and we headed back to our motel across the International Bridge, past dozens of unfortunate young boys standing in the ice-cold Rio Grande River holding long poles with cardboard cones on top, begging for coins to be tossed down to them.

Sometime in the early morning hours we three girls awakened to the sound of a guitar and *Slow Poke* in the same, but even raspier voice than the one we had heard in Juarez. Marn whispered, "Babs, Connie, wake up! Did you hear that?"

"Hear what?" I replied sleepily.

"The music, silly," Connie added. "They're next door. Let's go!" We threw on our clothes as fast as we could.

"I'll call the guys and tell them to meet us there," I said.

Harold replied, "We're on our way."

Uncle Alton and his brother-in-law had gone back after the show to bribe the western singer with money and a full bottle of Jack Daniel's whiskey, and brought him to our motel. We all sat around requesting songs and singing along to *Slow Poke*.

Our cowboy singer would stop now and then to tip the bottle and remind his kidnappers that he had to be back in Juarez in time for the two o'clock matinee floorshow. Mama finally declared, "It's time to go to bed. We have to get up early and prepare the horses for the parade." That was the last we saw of our whiskey-drinking cowpoke until he became a well-known television star a few years later.

The parade and football game were all right, but anticlimactic compared to the New Year's Eve party the night before. We went back across the bridge to Juarez again the next night, but left early since Alton's brother-in-law smarted off to a policeman and Dad and Alton had to go "talk" and "pay" him out of jail, or he would probably still be there.

I had a whirlwind courtship with Harold. I met him on a double-date when I was with his best friend, Norman. We went to a movie and later saw each other on a few more double dates. Somehow I started dating Harold instead of Norman. Our parents had gone to school together years before. His family were farmers and had been in the Pecos Valley almost as long as mine, so we had quite a lot in common. Harold was a student at NMMI, but was a

Roswell boy so we attended both the Roswell High School and New Mexico Military Institute social events together.

His cousin, Wayne, flew him out to the ranch one summer afternoon for a visit. I saw the yellow Piper Cub flying over as I was out riding Blanco. I had my shirt off getting a tan, so I hurriedly tied the reins together and headed the horse toward the house in a gallop, as I quickly put my shirt back on. I rode up just as they landed. We had a glass of cool lemonade at the house before they made a hair-raising take-off, just barely missing the top of the rocky hills surrounding the house. My father said, "Never again!"

The next time my beau called at the ranch that summer, he came by car. He had a broken foot in a cast, so his buddy, Norman, drove for him. They arrived just as it was getting dark. Norman stayed in the living room visiting with my parents, while Harold and I went outside to talk.

My sweetheart pulled out an engagement ring and asked, "Will you marry me?" while we were standing out in the moonlight between the garage and the old "two-holer." We returned to the house where I showed my folks my ring. Mama smiled and nodded her consent. I think she had already seen that we were in love. I don't recall Dad saying anything, even though he and Mother both liked Harold. Tom didn't tease me until Harold and Norman had driven off in the dark. For once, Mama told him, "Leave Barbara alone."

We had gone to bed as soon as Harold and Norman left. It was past nine o'clock, my father's bedtime. Sometime several hours later I heard a knock on the kitchen door. No one knocked at ranches,

Just married

but no one ever came to the door that late at night either. Dad went to see who it was. It was Norman, who had walked several miles from where he had driven their car into a small mud hole; it was stuck. He had to walk to get help since Harold was on crutches.

Norman had followed the long winding road all the way in the dark. My father dressed and took the truck to pull the two boys out of the mud hole. It was almost daylight when he returned, so he started cooking breakfast as soon as he got back home. Dad woke all of us up early. He was not in a good mood. I was embarrassed, but not nearly as badly as my fiancée and Norman were.

My brother Tom made sure a couple of my boisterous male cousins had heard the story about Harold's proposal near the "outhouse" by the time school started in the fall. They were ready when they saw me coming. "Hey, Babs, I hear you and Harold got engaged in the privy." I was still on such a cloud with my sparkling new diamond ring and so much in love, their taunts didn't even bother me.

Harold graduated from NMMI in early June. Dad had decided to mark lambs the following day. Mama let me stay in town at Grandma Long's, so I could attend the graduation ceremony only on the condition that I get up early and be at the ranch to round up sheep no later than five o'clock the next morning. Of course I agreed.

Somehow I persuaded Grandma that I should be allowed to spend the night with my friend Alice. My grandmother knew of my plans to go to the ranch early to help work stock the following day. What she didn't know was that Harold and I planned to drive to Carlsbad, a little over an hour away, and get married right after the graduation ceremony. Harold's sister, Janet, and Norman were both in on our elopement plans, and were going along to stand up for us.

I arrived at the ranch the next morning, worked all day, and didn't tell my parents that I was now a married woman. My husband came to the ranch a few days later and announced our marriage. Dad shook his hand and pulled out his checkbook. He had told me years before that I had the choice between a large formal wedding or the money that would be saved if I should choose to elope.

Dad's word was always good.